HOW TO CONTROL REAL ESTATE AGENTS

NEIL JENMAN
(Australia's trusted real estate author)

HOW TO CONTROL REAL ESTATE AGENTS

with
Alec Jenman

How To Control Real Estate Agents
By Neil Jenman

Published by Authors First
25/7 Anella Avenue Castle Hill NSW 2154 Australia
Telephone (02) 98946265
©Neil Jenman 2025
First Published in Australia in 2025

All rights reserved. No part of this publication may be reproduced, stored in a retrieval system, or transmitted, in any form or by any means, electronic, mechanical, photocopying, recording or otherwise, without the prior permission of the publishers.

Printed in Australia by McPhersons
Cover Design Victoria Zelenyuk
Layout by Gr8 Graphics

National Library of Australia, Cataloguing-in-Publication entry:
- Jenman, Neil

ISBN   9781763624504

Dedicated with immense pride to
HAROLD EDGAR LANYON
who detested shirkers

And, as always, for my darling wife,
Reiden Jenman
whose love, loyalty and support never wavers.

And in memory of Barney Allam OAM who sadly died August 4, 2024. If real estate agents had the integrity of Barney, this book would not be needed. Thank you for the many lives you touched so positively, including mine.

"The worst stress in life comes from being trapped in situations over which we have no control."

Neil Jenman

"NON DUCOR DUCO."
[I am not led, I lead.]

MESSAGE FROM AUTHOR
CONTROL AND POWER:
IT'S ABOUT WHAT YOU KNOW AND WHAT YOU DO

Thank you for starting this book. If you stick with me, you'll have the best chance of getting the best price with low costs and low stress when you sell your home. When you keep control instead of surrendering it, you also have fun. Or, at least, you enjoy selling a home.

Control makes you feel good, it gives you confidence – especially if you're dealing with someone from the least trusted profession, a real estate agent.

So, let's dispel a myth now: It's not "a few rotten apples" that give good agents a bad name; the entire real estate industry is rotten.

As you are about to read, unethical conduct is taught to agents; it's in the DNA of their systems, all of which are designed to control clients. Many bosses and major networks now insist their agents use unethical strategies to push their own insidious agendas.

Therefore, the majority of unethical agents give the ethical minority a bad name.

> It's not "a few rotten apples" that give good agents a bad name; the entire real estate industry is rotten.

There is one way to pick the difference between unethical agents (the majority) and decent agents (the minority). The bad guys want to control you. Good agents never try to control you.

All you have to do is read their listing agreements (carefully and slowly) before you sign up with them – and you'll see what I mean.

If you sign an agent's selling agreement without deleting all their nasty control clauses, you're toast. It's that simple.

But don't worry, I'll help you. In my role of supporting home sellers, I regularly help sellers achieve hundreds of thousands of dollars – sometimes millions – more for their homes.

The saying "knowledge is power" has never been truer than when selling your biggest asset. Knowledge gives you the power to control agents instead of being controlled by agents.

Provided, of course, that you act upon the knowledge you acquire.

You have my promise that I will show you how to keep control when selling any property. All I ask is that you "stick with me" – as good friends say to one another.

> Knowledge gives you the power to control agents instead of being controlled by agents.

INTRODUCTION

REAL ESTATE CAN BRING OUT THE WORST IN PEOPLE

Since my first day in real estate, as a 17-year-old in a small agency in a small Central Queensland town,[1] I have tried to do good. Not just for me, but for sellers and buyers who have given me the honour of their trust.

I vowed to do two things: *Work hard and take care of clients.*

To me, success in real estate means being trusted. But, as my friend Michael Kies reminds me: *"Real estate can bring out the worst in people."*

In 1992, I was at a conference in California. I met an Australian agent.[2] We sat together during lectures. Afterwards we went sight-seeing. Upon check-out, the agent's credit card was maxed-out. He asked for my help. I paid his account on my card and he wrote me a cheque for the amount he borrowed. Back in Australia I banked his cheque. It bounced. His response, I "took too long to bank it". When I spread this story, he threatened me.

Another agent[3] – a supposed friend – was headed to the United States. He came to my home and asked if I had any American currency. I gave him $870 in US notes. He promised to repay me on his return. That was in 1994. He has never repaid a cent. He says the exchange rate with America has not been good enough. In 30 years, sure.

Years later, a group of grateful agents offered to take me to dinner. It was my birthday. Thirty of us met at Melbourne's famed Chinese restaurant *The Flower Drum*. At the end of the night – after the agents departed – the waiter approached. I thought he had come to wish me well. But no. He gave me a bill for $5270. As my wife and I walked home, I felt like crying.

In about 2014, an agent[4] who regularly attended my courses developed cancer. Our home in Melbourne is near the respected Peter MacCallum Cancer Centre. My wife and I allowed this agent and his wife to live in our home for six months. Rent-free. Three years later, he ripped us off for $42,000.

Consider this: If agents cheat me – with my decades of experience – imagine how easily they cheat the public?! If the world's biggest real estate crook[5] can snare the US presidency, what chance is there for inexperienced consumers? Beware the ubiquity of con artists.

> If agents cheat me – with my decades of experience – imagine how easily they cheat the public?!

The real estate industry resembles the lawlessness of Australia's frontier. Dishonesty is everywhere. The authorities rarely prosecute law-breaking agents. There is a massive dichotomy between the appearance and the reality of real estate.

I am not an agent. I sold my agency in the 1990s when I began teaching agents systems based on client care. It's a philosophy that gave my agency phenomenal success.

Over the years, thousands of agents attended my courses. Yet to my frustration few followed my methods. Sure, agents would swear allegiance to "The Jenman System". But soon, they'd revert to what was easy and unethical.

In 2019, I ceased supporting all but a few agents. I was sick of being let down. Or perhaps, as I often tell myself, I am not good enough at persuading agents that goodness is the best way to succeed in life – if true happiness, not crass hedonism, is their measure of success.

Having written several books for consumers which were well received, I did what I should have done earlier. I devoted my working life to supporting home sellers.

In 2020, after he left school, I was joined by my son Alec. He often says I take my work too seriously and I worry too much. But when I see thousands of sellers ripped off by agents using systems that benefit agents, it almost makes me feel ill.

My life would be easier if I accepted today's real estate world.

But to accept – and, worse, participate in – what happens in the current real estate world would mean that I would have to do what thousands of originally well-meaning agents do – cross to the dark side. And that I will never do.

If I stopped fighting to protect consumers – and acceded to the wishes of the real estate industry – it would make me ashamed. To me, shame is the worst type of failure.

My dear wife, Reiden, says that "trust is more important than love". She's right. I love being trusted by good and decent home sellers and buyers.

I hope I can win (or keep) your trust too. Most of all, I hope this book gives you the confidence to control real estate agents.

Thank you for your interest.

My best wishes to you.

Neil Jenman – 2025

WARNING
THE TRAGEDY OF STUBBORN SELLERS

Sellers who demand too high a price usually end up selling for too low a price. They don't realise it – especially at the start – but they severely damage the value of their homes by demanding too much when they first list their homes for sale.

This book will help you get the best price when you sell a property. It will not create miracles. Some sellers don't need an agent, they need a magician. These are the stubborn sellers.

If you have a lovely home, of course you should get the best price. If you control the process. But being in control does not mean being stubborn. If you hold out too long you will surely sell too low.

No one can pick the high or low of a market. No one can control a market. All they can do is get the best price in the market in which they buy or sell.

Getting the best price is an outcome you can control.

If your home is for sale for more than a few weeks and no one buys it, there can only be two reasons (or a combination of both): Either your price is too high, or your agent is too incompetent. Stubborn sellers always blame agents.

But, regardless of the reason, here's the danger: If your home is unsold for too long, buyers think the price is too high or something is wrong with your home.

And then low offers come. Time usually forces prices down.

Here is a common tragedy: Sellers list with an agent. Their property does not sell because they reject the early offers and, maybe, the agent's advice.

They change agents.

The second (or third) agent sells their home for less than the price obtained by the first agent. Those early offers can be the best offers.

If you do everything right – and your home doesn't sell – you must reduce your price expectations. This does not mean you "lose". Expectations are not assets. You can't lose what you never had.

To get the best price, be the best seller – in information, in control and in being smart. Not stubborn.

A huge part in getting the best price is keeping control of the sale process.

TABLE OF CONTENTS

Message from author vii

Introduction ix

Warning xii

PART 1 – Most agents can't be trusted 1
Two Important Points to Get the Best Results
Three Challenges for Agents
Agents Commission
How Agents are Forced to be Dishonest

PART 2 – How home sellers can control the sales process 10
Imagine if you could do the following:

- ✓ *Force agents to honour price quotes.*
- ✓ *Force agents to release you from the Selling Agency Agreement*
- ✓ *Force agents to only charge you once your home is sold.*
- ✓ *Force agents to allow you to sell to a relative or friend.*
- ✓ *Force agents to allow any agents to show your home to buyers.*
- ✓ *Force agents to never under-quote your home.*

Four basic consumer rights 13

Three ways to sell your property 14
First way to sell: A typical agent
Second way to sell: Do it yourself
Third way to sell: A good agent

PART 3 – 27 ways sellers can control agents 19

PART 4 – 11 top tips for a top result 77

PART 5 – 15 points of caution 93

PART 6 – Extra control	125
32 Questions	135
Insist on protection and support	142
A brief summary of how to control real estate agents	145
Afterword	148
Advice to agents	150
Join us at Jenman	152
Words from a few sellers	153
Acknowledgements	157
Source notes	159
About the authors	173
Publications	174
Index	175

PART 1

MOST AGENTS CAN'T BE TRUSTED

"If you make yourself a sheep, the wolves will eat you."

Ben Franklin

TWO IMPORTANT POINTS TO GET THE BEST RESULT

POINT 1: PROTECTION CONTROL

Before you sign up with an agent, be sure you are protected from common traps that catch most sellers. The two most critical protection conditions – like seat belts and air bags in a car – are to be sure you do not pay (or are not liable to pay) any commission or marketing costs to the agent until your house is sold and you are happy with the price and the result. The second protection condition is to be sure you can ESCAPE if you are unhappy with the agent. Never sign a long-term locked-in listing contract.[6]

POINT 2: PERFORMANCE CONTROL

Once you have protection control, hopefully the agent's performance will exceed your expectations. The agent needs to be a skilled salesperson, one who can focus on getting buyers to pay their highest price, not pushing you to accept your lowest price. The agent must be a skilled negotiator. The agent must not damage the value of your home, as commonly happens with so many homes offered for sale. To get the best result you and/or your agent must protect the value of your home.

ALWAYS REMEMBER:

> Better to spend three or four weeks
> searching for the right agent
> than three or four months
> controlled by the wrong agent.

CONTROL ALERT
THE SEVEN-WORD SAFETY QUESTION

Many years ago, I learned a seven-word "safety question".

Before making any decision of any consequence, especially when asked to sign anything, you *always* ask yourself this seven-word question.

"What is the worst that can happen?"

During my adult life, asking (and answering) this seven-word question BEFORE deciding has saved me massive financial loss plus prevented needless emotional pain. This question can do the same in your life.

Property sellers who sign up with agents seldom realise how much control they give to the agent. So, for your own sake – both financially and emotionally – start by remembering three words (that I have been screaming aloud for decades):

DON'T SIGN ANYTHING![7]

At least until you are sure you are safe with the best chance of the best result.

What follows is intended to scare you (as it should, because so many home sellers are traumatised financially and emotionally when dealing with real estate agents). It's a summary of 13 unfair conditions* contained in many (if not most) of the Selling Agency Agreements (legally binding contracts) that agents get sellers to sign when listing their homes for sale. Agents are notorious for downplaying the dangers of this unfair "agreement".

If you sign this agreement, you lose control of the sale of your home. From the moment you sign, you are controlled by the agent with whom you signed.[8]

Once you follow the control points in this book, you will have control over any agent.

And that's the way it should be.

GOOD NEWS
Sellers can
KEEP CONTROL
by
deleting nasty clauses
and
adding nice clauses.

And, of course, by vowing to never sign legally binding documents – especially with members of the least trusted profession (real estate agents) – without INDEPENDENT LEGAL ADVICE. Or at least get help from someone who knows what they are doing. Someone who cares about you more than the agent. Remember, agents want you to sign up and to control you.

To be controlled, or not to be controlled, begins with your signature.

You can control what you sign and when you sign.

DON'T SIGN ANYTHING!

With a typical agent without crossing out their unfair and nasty clauses.*

*See Caution Point Number 1 in Part 5 of this book.

THREE CHALLENGES
FOR AGENTS

1. FINDING SELLERS

Unlike most businesses, agents must find their stock. All agents are eager to win the rights to sell your home – it's called "listing" your home.

This is when you have the best chance to secure control. Act now and keep control. If not, if you just sign up as the agent suggests, you will lose control.

2. SIGNING UP (and CONTROLLING) SELLERS

This is where sellers make their biggest mistake. If you choose the wrong agent, you will have more stress, more expenses, and a lower price.

Better to spend weeks searching for the best agent than months stuck with the wrong agent. Once you sign up with agents, you are "tied up". You'll be a "controlled listing".

But when you understand the real estate world, you can control agents instead of agents controlling you.

3. SELLING THE HOME

Having listed a home, agents have a problem: sellers who want too much.

But these agents have control over sellers. So begins what's known as "conditioning". Everything the agents do once they sign up sellers has one aim – to persuade the sellers to lower their price so their homes can easily sell.

Most agents are skilled at conditioning sellers down in price.

AGENTS' COMMISSION

As real estate has boomed, so have agents' commissions.

When I sold homes in the 1990s, my average commission was $3500. Today, in the same area, the average commission is $25,000.[9]

That's a seven-fold increase in barely 20 years.

Considering it takes (on average) less than 10 hours' "work" to sell a home and considering that salespeople earn as much as $50,000 to "sell" one home, it's easy to see how the industry attracts people who are greedy and lazy.

The word to remember with agents' commission is: **JUSTIFY**.

Can you *justify* paying someone tens of thousands of dollars to "sell" your home?

In the right cases, with the right agents, the answer may be "yes".

In the following pages, you will see what is meant by "right cases".

You will also discover how to find the "right agent". If not (if you can't find the right agent), you can sell without an agent.

Don't think you have no choice. You have many choices in real estate, especially when you keep control, when you don't give your power away.

So, if you cannot justify paying a stranger tens of thousands of dollars to "sell" your home, surely you should consider selling without an agent.[10]

Most home sellers are more than capable of doing the same – or better – than most agents!

How's that for a claim?

As you're about to discover, it's true.

Control can be yours. Control must be yours. Control gives you the power to choose.

Best of all, control gets you the best result.

****

HOW AGENTS ARE FORCED TO BE DISHONEST

"I can't understand how ethics in real estate can work."
Email to author from agent[11]

A moral dilemma faces all agents. If they are honest, they risk going broke.

Here's what commonly happens …

When owners want to sell, they call three agents. When each agent arrives, owners ask two questions:

Question 1: *How much is my property worth?*

Question 2: *How much is your commission?*

Regardless of how they dance around the topic, most agents know that if they tell you the truth, they will lose your business. To quote Leonard Cohen: *"I told the truth and look where it got me."*[12]

Say your home is worth $2 million. Like most owners, you have a high opinion of your home. This is the "endowment principle" – the tendency to overvalue assets to which we are emotionally attached.

So, you may think your home is worth as much as $2.5 million.

Let's look at how the three agents may respond:

Agent Number 1 is honest. She says, *"Your home is worth around $2 million."* You are shocked. Maybe offended. Clearly, she can't see the true worth of your home.

And so, Agent 1 gets rejected.

Agent Number 2 seems optimistic. He feels you'll get "over $2 million". Although he doesn't say how much, he does offer to cut his commission. Things look better now.

Agent 2 is told that you will consider him.

Agent Number 3 arrives. This bloke claims to be the "top agent". Although he talks about himself more than about your home, you are drawn in. Especially when he mentions the price. Agent 3 loves your home. He says buyers will fall over themselves to buy your home. He says he wouldn't be surprised if you get $2.5 million – "maybe more if marketed right".

Oh wow, this sounds good. And what does "marketed right" mean? you ask.

Agent 3 gives you the pitch that makes owners sign up. *"The best way to sell is auction,"* says Agent 3. *"Get all buyers together, let them fight it out. Watch the price go up and up. Fantastic."*

Agent 3 gives you stunning success stories. He tells you about sellers who wanted $3 million for their home and sold by auction for $4.2 million.

It all sounds so simple, so exciting. Agent 3 seems the obvious choice.

You agree to pay $10,000 for marketing.[13]

You sign up with Agent Number 3. You are now under the complete control of Agent 3. No matter how he treats you, no matter what he tells you about price, once you sign up, you are locked up.

If you try to escape, you will likely:

- Be forced to pay two commissions. One to Agent 3 who did not sell your home and one to the agent who does sell your home.
- If you refuse to pay those needless "marketing costs", you may find a caveat on your home.
- Your home (if not sold at auction) becomes an "Auction Lemon". It's a reject.

But let's say you do decide – as happens with thousands of sellers – to sell *at* the auction. Auction agents are trained to persuade sellers to lower their reserve price, especially in the high pressure of an auction.

As one manual teaches agents:

> *"Move quickly. They are usually numb.*
> *Don't give them time to dwell on the price."*[14]

Your home sells at auction for $1.7 million.

Although disappointed, you smile sheepishly as the crowd claps. You are relieved that the ordeal is over.

Most people do not realise the huge stress and emotional pressure placed on home sellers. Conditioning is no joke. It's a cruel control process that forces prices down by breaking the resolve of sellers.

Meanwhile Agent Number 1 learns what happened to you at the auction. She says to herself: *"I lost that listing because I quoted the sellers $2 million. It then gets sold at auction for at least $300,000 less than I could have achieved. I lost the commission, but the sellers lost a lot more by underselling."*

Agent Number 1 got punished for being honest.

Agent Number 3 got rewarded for being dishonest.

So, what will Agent Number 1 do next time she meets prospective sellers?

Now you know why agents feel forced to be dishonest.

If they're not dishonest, most agents will go broke. Being dishonest is how agents win control.

Selling real estate is all about control.

PART 2

HOW HOME SELLERS CAN CONTROL THE SALES PROCESS

MAKE AGENTS
AN OFFER THEY CAN'T REFUSE.
Such as: "If you want a big commission,
don't attempt to condition or control us,
just get us the best price and treat us well."

This can be one of the first statements you make when you meet an agent. And then, if necessary, repeat this statement until the agent agrees in words and *actions* to accept your reasonable offer.

IMAGINE IF YOU COULD DO THE FOLLOWING:

✓ *Force agents to honour price quotes.*

If an agent quotes a selling price before you sign up and then, after you sign up, the agent pushes you to accept a lower price, the agent will forfeit their right to commission.

If you feel this is unrealistic or unfair, consider this: Why are selling prices always less than quoted prices? The answer is obvious: Agents deliberately "over-quote" to win listings.

It's called: "BUYING THE LISTING".

✓ *Force agents to release you from the Selling Agency Agreement.*

If you sign up with an agent because they seem competent and caring but then, after you sign up, they become incompetent and uncaring – or, worse, dishonest – you should have the right to cancel the agency agreement without any penalty or further cost or obligation. In the typical real estate world, however, once you sign up, you are stuck with the agent.

✓ *Force agents to only charge you once your home is sold.*

Thousands of sellers fail to sell their homes. Mostly because they resist pressure to drop their price. But these sellers are usually out-of-pocket several thousand dollars – mostly for marketing expenses that benefited agents. As you'll read in Control Point 10, agents con sellers into promoting agents. Further, they use the sellers' money to source new leads for themselves.[15]

✓ *Force agents to allow you to sell to a relative or friend.*

Many times, after sellers sign up, a friend or relative (even a neighbour) offers to buy their home. Even if the agent has done no work, sellers are legally bound to pay full commission regardless of who buys their home. But, if you have control, you can force the agent to charge you nothing, especially if the agent has done nothing and you sell the home yourself.

✓ *Force agents to allow any agents to show your home to buyers.*

In the typical real estate world, an "Exclusive Agreement" is really an "excluded agreement". By signing up with one agent you exclude other agents from showing your home.

In the United States, for example, when you list with one agent, all the agents can show your home.[16]

✓ *Force agents to never under-quote your home.*

It's called "low-balling" and it's a common trick.

Incredibly, some sellers sanction this trick. Agents tell sellers that if they "quote a low price", it attracts more buyers. And it does. If your home is offered below its value, you will attract more buyers.

But, at what price? A lower price, of course.

The agent then says, *"This is what the market is telling you."*

Get real: The agent has been searching in the wrong market.

> **The agent has been searching in the *wrong* market.**

Do not allow agents to "low-ball" the price of your home.

Please understand this important control point: Sellers do not have to accept being told *"This is the way we do it"*.

When you understand how you should sell your home, you can instruct the agent with confidence. You can keep control.

You will then get a better result.

CONSUMER RIGHTS

In the early 1960s, governments began to focus upon four main consumer rights.[17]

Incredibly, these rights are barely available to real estate consumers. To retain control, make sure you obtain your basic rights.

4 BASIC CONSUMER RIGHTS

1. THE RIGHT TO SAFETY

Home sellers are not safe when they sign up with a typical agent.

As you will see in the section 13 UNFAIR CLAUSES THAT CATCH SELLERS, typical Selling Agreements protect agents, not sellers.

2. THE RIGHT TO BE INFORMED

Real estate consumers are deliberately misinformed. There are many reasons that real estate agents are the least trusted businesspeople in our society. One reason is the flood of lies and deceit agents habitually spread.

3. THE RIGHT TO CHOOSE

As most sellers soon discover, when they call out three agents, it's as if they called the same agent three times. Same pitch, different faces. You are given one way only. Usually, the choice you are offered is not the best choice for you. In some areas, agents collude to set commissions at an inflated rate.[18]

4. THE RIGHT TO REDRESS (GUARANTEE)

You get more guarantees when you hire a plumber to unblock a drain than when you hire a typical agent to sell your home. If you are naïve enough to sign up with an agent without insisting on a guarantee, you will get ripped off. For sure, no buts or maybes.

> You get more guarantees when you hire a plumber.

3 WAYS TO SELL YOUR HOME

Most homeowners think there is one way to sell a home: Contact a few agents and sign up with one. But there are three ways to sell your home.

FIRST WAY TO SELL: **A TYPICAL AGENT**

Networks, institutes or trainers train most agents. The training focuses upon: *How to do what's best for the agent* – not the sellers.

And that means how to exploit, manipulate, charge and control sellers.

The most important skill for agents is: *How to sign up sellers.* It is *not* how to negotiate the best price for listings.

Most sellers do not realise: Once you sign up with a typical agent, you will pay thousands of dollars if you sell or not.

Most agents want to earn a lot for doing a little.

Listings, listings, listings – that's the real estate agency world.

Agents have a saying: *"CONTROL THE LISTINGS AND YOU CONTROL THE SALES."*

"Controlled" home sellers finish up with three outcomes:

> First Outcome: They pay thousands of dollars for needless costs.
>
> Second Outcome: Their homes are short sold.
>
> Third Outcome: They pay too much commission.

BUT …

It does not have to be this way.

From signing you up to a legal **contract** to getting you to lower your price through "conditioning", everything is designed to control you. Eventually, you are worn down – emotionally and professionally – and you sell at any price.

All sellers start off believing they can resist the methods of typical agents. But most sellers capitulate in a few weeks – three months at most.

The way to protect yourself is to control the agent instead of the agent controlling you.

If you can't find an agent who offers you risk-fee selling, you must consider the second way to sell.

SECOND WAY TO SELL: **DO IT YOURSELF**

Consider what typical agents do and you'll realise there is nothing that most sellers – with reasonable intelligence – cannot do themselves.

Look at what typical agents do ...

• ADVERTISING

Agents ask you to pay money to advertise to find buyers.

Surely you can place your own ads. Find buyers yourself. You will not have to pay huge advertising costs PLUS huge commission costs. And often you'll get a better price.[19]

Are you capable of placing an ad for your home? Obviously, yes. Easily.

• INSPECTIONS (Waiting for buyers)

Once a typical agent advertises your home, that agent sits at your home (okay, some stand – and some fall asleep) for about 30 minutes each week waiting for buyers.

Consider this: Each week has 10,080 minutes. A typical agent "opens" your home for 30 minutes. What business closes 99.5 percent of each week? It's madness.

Here's another question: *Could you sit at your home and wait for buyers to inspect it?* Of course. And you'd make your home available for more than 30 minutes a week.

• NEGOTIATION

Surely, you may think, agents can negotiate. That's why you need an agent. No, most agents are hopeless at negotiating. Their forte is conditioning you down in price.[20]

YOU CAN DO WHAT TYPICAL AGENTS DO. If you can't find a good agent, you may as well do it yourself – or at least have a go. You'll have nothing to lose and plenty to save.

THIRD WAY TO SELL: **A GOOD AGENT**

A good agent is the best way to sell your home.

Good agents pay for themselves. They get you the best price with the least costs and stress.

Unfortunately, good agents are hard to find.

To find a good agent, you need to recognise good agents.

There are two parts to a good agent – PERSONAL and PROFESSIONAL.

Are they decent human beings? Do you feel you can trust them? Are they the sort of person you'd be comfortable inviting for dinner?

> Good agents pay for themselves.

Believe it, character is important. If you hire an agent of integrity, you will be treated well.

Now, please remember: It's impossible for an agent to treat you honestly if they use systems built on dishonesty.

Therefore, you need to find an agent who is different from most agents, who will place your interests ahead of their interests, OR you must force a typical agent to place your interests first.

First, let's look at how you can recognise a good agent.

ON A PERSONAL LEVEL

Good agents are well-presented. They turn up on time; they are polite.

Good agents take a genuine interest in your home. They want to know what makes your home special and what you may love about your home.

Good agents say good things – so will bad agents, so be careful. However, when good agents say something good, they back it up. They walk their talk. For example, if an agent says they place your interests first (as most claim), it won't take long to expose the bad agents by asking questions such as: *"How is this in my best interests?"*

Once you understand how agents operate, you will be confident of controlling agents instead of having agents control you. You might also have fun.

Being competent gives you confidence.

ON A PROFESSIONAL LEVEL

This is where you instantly spot good agents or bad agents.

Here is how the good agents operate ...

NO RISK

All business involves risk. Good agents accept risk; it's the price of earning a profit. Bad agents pass risk to sellers. Amazingly, many sellers accept. But not you.

Good agents charge nothing until your property is sold.

And charging "nothing" means exactly that – *nothing*. The agent will cover all costs that may be incurred with the sale of your home, except, of course, specific home improvements costs. All marketing costs are included in the commission or only payable once your home is sold.

With typical agents (bad agents), sellers often pay thousands of dollars and don't sell their homes. To profit from the losses of clients is highly unethical.

Good agents will never profit from your losses.

Good agents have a "no charges until sold" policy.

The GOLDEN RULE when selling any property is this:

NEVER PAY

ANY MONEY

TO ANY AGENT

BEFORE YOU SELL!

NO AUCTIONS

The surest way to detect bad agents are those who say auction is the best way to sell. These agents are crooks or idiots – or both.

Auction is the worst way to sell any home at any time.

Good agents never do auctions to sellers. Auctions are a financial assault on home sellers. If you doubt this claim, read my book *88 Reasons Why You Must Never Auction Your Home*.[21]

QUALIFIED AND IDENTIFIED

Good agents ensure that people who inspect your home are qualified and identified. Good agents shy away from free-for-all "open houses". They do not let unidentified strangers wander through your home. Sticky-beaks, nosy neighbours, tyre-kickers and, worst of all, burglars "casing" your home for a later robbery, are not welcome in your home.

> **Ensure that people who inspect your home are qualified and identified.**

GUARANTEE

Good agents offer a guarantee. If something goes wrong – or they do wrong – you can dismiss them. You are not "locked in". You have control, not the agent. You can escape.[22]

PART 3

27 WAYS SELLERS CAN CONTROL AGENTS

CONTROL WAY 1
YOU KNOW – and they know you know!

Act confident. Agents need to see you as informed.

They should know that you know how to get the best result for yourself without needless expenses.

Most agents rely on the lack of knowledge of home sellers.[23]

> When agents know that you are well informed, you have control.

BUT as soon as agents know you are informed, they will fear you or get angry or churlish – at least that's what the worst agents will do.

BUT good agents – even some bad ones – will respect you for having the sense to have done your research before you sell.

When agents know that you are well informed, you have control.

CONTROL WAY 2
THE POWER OF YOUR KNOWLEDGE
– Fair, firm and friendly

It can be tempting to mock or humiliate agents when you know their tricks and secrets. But there is no real benefit in being rude. Agents work harder when you are fair. As military leaders know, it's important to be "fair, firm and friendly" when encouraging people.

Make it clear that all you want is to *sell your home for the best market price* without incurring needless costs or putting yourself at risk of losing (or wasting) money.

You don't expect miracles, but you won't accept being treated like most sellers. Most importantly, you will not relinquish control of your valuable asset to a real estate agent.

As many knowledgeable sellers attest, they soon have typical agents stumbling and stuttering.

You should be able to persuade agents that hard work, risk-taking (on their part) and placing your interests first, is the best way to win the right to sell your home.

Always remember the great incentive – the large commission the agent will earn if they sell your home for the best possible price.

Your knowledge of the workings of the industry plus your firmness and courtesy towards the agent will give you control of the agent and the sale process.

CONTROL WAY 3
BE SERIOUS
Your home *will be* SOLD

The keener you are to sell, the keener agents will be to work for you.

Never say to agents:

"We don't need to sell."

OR

"We won't give it away."

OR

"We'll wait for our price."

Agents hear such statements constantly. Even if you feel this way, don't say it. It will deflate them.

> The keener you are to sell, the keener agents will be to work for you.

Agents worry about three factors: Money, time and reputation.

If agents think they may lose their own money (on advertising) and waste their time (trying to sell an overpriced home) and then, if they fail, you'll be unhappy (and go elsewhere and sell for less), they will lose interest.

But if agents believe you are a serious seller, and they will get a large commission – plus costs reimbursed *when* you sell – they will be keen to be your agent.

You must dangle a carrot in front of them (dollars in commission).

Aside from wanting to know the lowest price you will take (don't tell them!), agents are eager to know "how motivated" you are to sell.

To control the agent, you must let them know:

"We are keen to sell."

Better still, if you say these five words, agents will be excited.

"THIS HOME WILL BE SOLD."

Once it's clear that you are a serious seller, then talk about commission.

CONTROL WAY 4
CONTROLLING COMMISSION
– Focus the right way, at the right time

Most sellers make a big mistake with commission when interviewing agents. One of the first things they do is ask how much commission agents charge; then they demand a discount.

This creates one of two outcomes:

Confrontation

The agent gets frustrated, and the sellers think the agent is greedy – which might be true, but this is not the time to negotiate commission.

Capitulation

If the first thing an agent does is agree to drop their commission, what will they do with your home? If agents can't negotiate a good commission for themselves, they'll unlikely negotiate a good price for your home.

> Cheap agents usually get cheap prices.

The simple truth is: Cheap agents usually get cheap prices.

So, what to do?

Simple – negotiate commission at point of sale, not at point of listing.

No matter how much agents "want" to be paid, no matter if they say they "don't negotiate their fee", remember this …

COMMISSION IS ALWAYS NEGOTIABLE.

But if you want the agent to work harder to get the best price, don't cut their commission *before* they make the sale. Your sale price is more important than their commission.

So, make it clear …

> *"If you get us the best price,*
> *we'll gladly pay you the best commission."*

Don't cut their commission *before* they make the sale.

Look how agents can view sellers who pay less commission. Say, an agent has two homes listed; both homes are similar, but one seller has cut the commission to 1.5 percent. The other seller will consider 2.5 percent (if they get the best price). If the agent only has one buyer, which home will the agent push? The one with the best commission or the one with the worst commission?

Here, again, is the BIG point about commission:

COMMISSION IS NEGOTIABLE RIGHT UP UNTIL THE POINT OF SALE.

To give you even more control, you can write the above words in the agent's agreement – preceded by the words, *"Agent agrees that …"*

When the agent brings a buyer, if you don't like the price, then negotiate commission.

ALWAYS FOCUS ON YOUR NET PRICE.

You don't pay the agent unless a sale happens.

Further, if the agent asks you to accept a lower sale price, you can ask the agent to accept a lower commission. But if you have already lowered the commission when you listed your home, you remove a major incentive to inspire the agent to get you a better sale price.

MORE IDEAS ABOUT CONTROLLING COMMISSION

• "THAT'S NET, RIGHT?"

No matter how much you are tempted to accept an offer, try one more idea to control the agent.

Say,

> *"We will accept this offer PROVIDED it's net."*

The agent will now go back to the buyers and negotiate to cover the commission. This means the agent is now negotiating for themself not you.

Believe it, they will try hard.[24]

> **The agent is now negotiating for themself.**

• "NEVER" IS NEVER TRUE

If an agent tells you they "never" reduce their commission, not for any sellers or for any reason, you can respond with the following questions:

"Have you ever reduced commission for any sellers?"

All agents have reduced commission at some stage in their lives. Why not for you?

"So, you'd rather get nothing than $25,000?" – or whatever they are demanding.

If their commission is, say, $35,000 and you want to pay $25,000, be clear that their choice is NOT between $25,000 and $35,000; it's between $25,000 and nothing.

Be determined to KILL THE SALE (agents hate that expression) than pay excessive commission.

Be fair. If the agent worked hard and got a great price, it's churlish to demand a discount.

> If the agent worked hard and got a great price, it's churlish to demand a discount.

• EXPOSE EXCESS

If you calculate commission on an hourly rate, it'll expose the excess. How much is a real estate agent worth?

Top barristers earn $1000 per hour. Neurosurgeons earn $500 per hour.

Most agents work less than 10 hours to "sell" a house. The average commission is about $25,000. Are agents 5 times better than neurosurgeons?

If they say they do lots of work for no pay, that's not your concern. You're paying for your home, nothing else.

• PAY FOR SKILL – not hours

Try not to think about hours worked. Instead, consider skill. Were you impressed with the agent's negotiating ability? Did the sale price exceed your expectations?

And a big one: *Was that price above or below the agent's quote before you listed?*

How do you feel: Elated, satisfied or miserable?

And the most important question: Was the skill of the agent the *sole reason* for a great price?

Be careful: Many agents credit themselves with achieving great prices when it was merely market forces. Agents praise themselves in a boom. But if prices fall, agents blame the market.

So, before you worry about commission, think about the agent's effort and effect on the final price. If you accept a price and the agent then negotiates more than you accepted, that's a good agent. Most agents stop trying once sellers accept an offer.

But remember, if you are going to negotiate the commission, do it before you agree on the final sale price. That's the point of sale.

Commission is always negotiable until the point of sale.

• JUSTIFY

A man had a dent in the fender of his flash car. A panel beater crawled under the car for two minutes. He then went to his workshop and grabbed a rubber hammer. He crawled back under the car and tapped. There was a pop and the dent disappeared. The owner was delighted.

The panel beater produced his invoice: $500.

The owner's delight turned to concern. *"Two minutes for one tap?!"*

The panel beater smiled: *"That's right, I charged $10 for the tap, and $490 for knowing where to tap."* The owner paid and drove away happily.

Can you justify the commission you are asked to pay?

With good agents, forget time. The agent may have spent years studying negotiation. The agent may know that typical real estate methods – like auctions, bait pricing and mass advertising – cause homes to undersell. If the agent's skill got you a few hundred thousand dollars – or millions of dollars – more for your home, the agent deserves a good commission.

• THE "POLICY" EXCUSE

Often, if you seek a benefit like a reduction in commission, agents cite "company policy" as an excuse for refusing. The word "policy" effectively shuts down a client's request.

But not with you.

Here's how you reply: *"You may have a company policy, but our family has a personal policy, and we can't go ahead without a discount."*

My wife and I once booked at a resort.[25] We thought it was awful. We decided to leave. The manager said, *"I don't think you are aware of our cancellation policy."* My wife replied, *"No, but I don't think you are aware of our expectation policy."* We departed with no penalty.

Your family's expectation policy should be that you insist on being treated fairly.

• BEWARE OF EXTRAS

It's a common trap. Sellers compare commission but ignore extras. An agent with a commission of 1 percent can cost more – with "extras" – than an agent who charges 2.5 percent.

Extra charges can exceed commission. Typically, extras are advertising (also called marketing, with surprise extras such as "copywriting" or absurdities such as "Chinese translation fee" or rip-off fees such as "administration fee") – most of which, as you will discover, are unnecessary.[26]

Australian agents are notorious for slugging sellers with "extra costs". In other countries, there is one cost for selling a house – commission. All extras – if any – are included in the commission, which is payable when a property is sold.

So, if an agent says you "must pay" for extra costs such as "marketing", make them aware that in other countries agents charge one fee – commission.

Ask an agent (who says marketing costs are essential): *"How do agents sell homes in America?"*

And then say: *"If advertising really does find a buyer, why do I need you? Why don't I advertise my own home and find that buyer? Why must I pay twice – for advertising and for commission?"*

• THE THIRD COST OF SELLING

There are three costs of selling a home. The first cost is commission. Rates vary from half a percent to four percent. On average, it's about 2 percent. The second cost is the "extras".

The third – and usually largest – cost is:

Underselling: Research shows that at least 90 percent of homes are undersold.[27]

> At least 90 percent of homes are undersold.

The difference between the amount buyers pay and the amount they are willing to pay – often hundreds of thousands of dollars – is the amount sellers lose. And most never know it.

The major reason for this third cost cannot be repeated too often: Most agents are hopeless negotiators. Oh sure, they have "been negotiating for years". But negotiating does not mean conditioning sellers. Or, as one trainer[28] teaches, *"You have to grind sellers down."* A grinder is not a negotiator. A negotiator sells a home for the highest price buyers will pay – not the lowest they can "grind" sellers down.

• THE BONUS COMMISSION

If you have a home worth, say, $2 million, how easy would it be to sell it for $1 million?

If an agent charges 2%, why should they get 2% ($20,000) on the first million? Ideally, if your home is worth $2 million – and you'd be happy at that price – an agent should be paid a small percentage (say, 0.5%) up to $2 million and a large percentage (say 25%) for every dollar above $2 million.

Several agents push this bonus method. Some sellers like it. The only danger is if sellers do not realise the value of their homes and they pay an agent a huge percentage for doing nothing other than selling at an easy-to-obtain price. If agents are dishonest and sellers are naïve, the bonus commission can be a major rip-off. Elderly sellers are vulnerable.

CONTROL WAY 5
TEST THE AGENT'S KNOWLEDGE

Does the agent know how to get you the best result?

The more knowledgeable an agent, the more you will get a better result – especially when it comes to negotiation. The agent must know how to persuade buyers to pay their best price.

I used to say to home sellers:

"There are two prices for every property – the price buyers want to pay and the price I can persuade buyers to pay."

You are not hiring an agent to find a buyer. Anyone can find a buyer – if your price is low.

Whether an agent sells a home for a high price or a low price, the agent gets a high commission.

There is a dreadful saying among agents – especially those you should avoid:

"Quote 'em low and watch 'em go. Quote 'em high and watch 'em die."

QUESTION to ask agents: *"What methods do you suggest to sell our home for the best price?"*

If they suggest any deception, they are the wrong agent.

BEWARE: Agents who suggests dishonest or ineffective methods are the wrong agents. The classic example of an ineffective method is public auction.

The reason agents push auctions is because, as one real estate institute course states:

"Auction is the fastest and best conditioning method." [29]

Do not ever put yourself in a position where an agent can control you.

Do not be timid about questioning agents. Agents who have a high level of knowledge relish the chance to share their expertise, especially when it's radically different from other agents – such as risk-free selling with a skilled negotiator. Typical agents will squirm and wriggle if you question their knowledge.

> Auction is the fastest and best conditioning method.

Some may even ask:

"What is this, a job interview?"

Yes, that's exactly what it is. You want to hire the best agent who can get the best price with no risk or needless expenses on your part. An agent where you keep control of the process.

TEST THEIR KNOWLEDGE and COMPETENCY.

The best way to measure the knowledge and competency of an agent is by discovering what they ***do*** and what they know, not what they ***say*** they do or what they claim to know.

You just need to ask simple but intelligent questions. Soon you'll discover which agents are the best.

Agents who are committed to being the best study their profession – as any good professional does. They attend courses, they read books, they travel, they study ethics and client care.

When I started in real estate, I attended every course available, I read every book I could find on real estate. I doubt there is a real estate book I have not read. I am still a prolific reader. As the great Australian journalist John Pilger urged everyone, especially those who must answer questions from well-informed people – "Read!"[30] The best agents are great readers.

QUESTION TO AGENT: *"Do you study real estate?"*

They will mention training courses they've attended – either by real estate institutes or trainers paid by advertisers (such as News Ltd). If this is all they've done, they will only have learned "how to condition sellers" *not* how to act ethically.

QUESTION TO AGENT (said with wry smile): *"Did you learn about 'conditioning'? Did you learn how to get VPA to increase your profile?"*

No agent can deny being taught tricks. You don't need to make them feel uncomfortable. It's sufficient that they know that you know what agents learn.

If you wish, you may add: *"We want an agent who won't use such tricks on us."*

YOUR KNOWLEDGE v THEIR KNOWLEDGE

Agents have had it too good too long. They have earned large commissions for doing little work. The longest boom in history had led to massive hubris in agents.

Agents know how to get maximum commission with minimum effort. By attending industry training courses, they learn to look after themselves. For example, one subject is called *"How to Protect Your Commission"*.[31]

If you have read any of my books, you will have a good understanding of how to protect yourself from the tricks in real estate and how to get the best result.

So, what do you do when agents you interview have not read any Jenman books? This means you surely have more knowledge than the agent. Even worse, it shows that the agent has not bothered to learn much about their craft. If they say – as some do – that they have "never heard of Jenman", it confirms their ignorance.

The Jenman philosophy can be summed up in one eight-word sentence:

The sellers' interests come before the agents' interests.

QUESTION TO AGENT: *"Have you read any of Neil Jenman's books?"*

If they say no, and if they are critical of me, you should ask: *"How can you be critical of an author whose books you haven't read?"*

NOTE: If you are using our support to help you with the sale of your property, we will express post a book to any agent you nominate.[32]

All agents are taught to put their own interests first.

You need an agent who has resisted typical methods and who welcomes the chance to treat you well.

But no matter what you think of the agent,
the most important point is this:

YOU MUST CONTROL THE AGENT
– **NOT** HAVE THE AGENT CONTROL YOU!

CAN'T DO IT HONESTLY: Incredibly, some agents are lost if they are asked to do real estate the right way – i.e. what's best for you. Minus their conditioning methods and tricks, they don't know what to do.

You must reject such agents.

ESSENTIAL KNOWLEDGE: If you are committed to getting the best result for you and your family, you need an agent who knows how to achieve such a result.

Here is the essential knowledge the agent needs to get you the best result:

<u>Knowing how to</u> protect the value of your home.

<u>Knowing how to</u> find buyers without wasting your money on needless advertising.

<u>Knowing how to</u> use the Rules of Real Estate Negotiation to get you the best price.

<u>Knowing how to</u> discover the Buyers' Highest Price – instead of focusing on your lowest price.

QUESTION TO AGENT: *"How do you plan to get us the best market price?"*

If you are not impressed with their reply, they are unlikely to be the right agent.

CONTROL WAY 6
SHORT-TERM SELLING AGREEMENTS

– Never allow yourself to be tied up for a long period

One of the main ways agents control sellers is through lengthy Selling Agency Agreements.

Most agents expect you to sign up for 90 days or 120 days. Some want 180 days.

Often, sellers don't realise – until after they sign up – how long they are locked up to the agent.

Here's the problem: If the agent proves to be no good – or if you don't like the agent – you cannot dismiss the agent. You can be controlled for months by a dishonest or incompetent agent.

It's easier to leave a bad life partner than to leave a bad agent. No matter what the agent does – or how the agent treats you – too bad. Once you sign up, you are tied up. This is what agents mean by "controlled listings".

Don't let yourself be controlled by an agent. Instead, make sure *you* control the agent.

Be careful you don't depress the agent.

Here's how you do it:
ONLY SIGN UP FOR 30 DAYS.
That's it.

If the agent squeals – as most will – say:

"Don't worry. We are happy to have you as our agent for however long it takes to get the best price; however, we will not sign up an agreement for more than a month. If we are happy with you, we will re-sign for another month at the end of each month."

As well as controlling the agent, be careful you don't depress the agent.

Make them believe you *will* keep them.

As explained in the next way – Control Way 7.

CONTROL WAY 7
ENCOURAGE AND REWARD EFFICIENCY

"Efficiency is doing better what is already being done."

Peter Drucker

Two important words to remember when dealing with agents: Efficient and Effective.

Plenty of agents are efficient – but at what? And for whom are they effective? Their usual efficiency involves controlling sellers and getting prices lowered – and that's not the most effective result for home sellers.

Here's a secret that few sellers either know or understand. Many times, as soon as your home is listed for sale, the agents know who's likely to buy it. Within hours, they are quite capable of selling your home at the best price to the best buyer. In doing so, not only can you get the best price but you also save thousands of dollars in needless "marketing" costs, plus weeks of stress.

But most agents won't do it.

Even if they keep great records and the exact buyer is known to them, they won't let your home be sold too quickly.

Why on earth not? you may ask.

Their reasoning is as simple as it is absurd: They're scared that you'll think they don't deserve a large commission for getting you a large price too quickly.

So, they control you – and attempt to justify their commission through an elaborate charade: multiple open houses (to find more leads for themselves), lots of advertising (at your expense) and then, finally, they will reveal the buyer they always knew about.

So, what would you prefer when selling your home? Would you like a great price within a week of listing? Or would you rather wait three months, spend thousands of dollars on needless advertising and sell for the same – or even a lower – price?

Imagine being sick and going to a doctor. You can be cured now or you can endure months of pain before you're cured – all for the same price. The choice is obvious.

So please, focus on the result you get. Never mind the time taken. Indeed, the less the time, the more efficient and effective the agent.

And surely that's worth extra commission not less.

Don't punish agents for being efficient if they get you a great price in a short time. Encourage them. Tell them you hope they sell your home quickly.

In the old days – when the quality of agents was higher – the first thing agents did when they listed a home was contact buyers known to the agents. Today, the first thing most agents do is charge sellers for expensive online ads. All to attract buyers already known to the agent.

Encourage your agent to be efficient and effective on your behalf. Show that you're in control and you know how the typical process works.

With you, there is no need for a charade of needless activity to justify a large commission. A large commission is what an agent can get if they sell your home for a large price.

And the sooner the better.

CONTROL WAY 8
STICK WITH THEM... IF...

– Inspire, don't threaten, the agent

No one likes to work under threat of dismissal.

Fear might control, but it rarely inspires.

So, to control and inspire ("condition") the agent, let them know that if they do the right thing, you will "stick with" them.

If the agent knows they will always be your agent – unless they do something dishonest (which good ones never intentionally do) – they will work hard for you. They will have no need to push you down in price because their time is running out.

Typically, with most agents, as their agreement nears expiry, the agents know they may be dismissed and the sellers may choose another agent (and sell for a lower price). The pressure is on them to sell your home before their time expires. So, they put you under pressure – and often damage your home's value – in their rush to get a sale before their listing expires.

> Fear might control, but it rarely inspires.

So, give them your solemn word that you will keep them as your agent – albeit on a month-to-month basis – until your home sells.

"Look after us and we will stick with you."

This will certainly control the agent and make them strive to get you the best price.

When a buyer makes a low offer, instead of urging you to take it, the agent can say to buyers:

"These sellers will stick with me, so if you don't pay them a fair (meaning 'high') price, I'll find them a buyer who will pay the right price."

And the agent – who is now more likely to be totally on your side and working hard for you – is likely to say to the buyers, especially those trying to buy cheaply:

"We are confident we will get the right price."

By bonding yourself to the agent, the agent will be on your side.

Hence the use of the word "WE".

As in: "WE WILL GET THE RIGHT PRICE."

CONTROL WAY 9
CONTROL "COMPARABLE CONDITIONING"

A common way agents condition and control home sellers is through "comparable sales". The agents produce a list of similar homes to yours.

All these homes will have been sold at prices lower than you hope to achieve.

Comparison control is powerful.

Agents use comparables as "proof" that their unsold homes need to be priced the same as sold homes.

But here's the point you need to understand – and perhaps you can also tell the agent.

As most (90%) homes are undersold, it means that most of the comparable homes you are shown have also been undersold.

And, given that the average amount by which homes are undersold is 10% of the price at which they were sold, this means that you need to...

ADD AT LEAST 10%
TO COMPARABLE SALES

If you are shown a property like yours and it sold for $1.5 million, it means this property should have sold for $1.65 million.

Or if you are shown a home that sold for $2 million, it will likely mean the buyers were willing to pay another 10%, being $2.2 million. That's $200,000 more.

Develop the habit of looking at comparable sales and asking: *What price should these homes have sold for?*

Or: *How much more were the buyers of these homes prepared to pay?*

When you see a comparable home to yours together with a stated selling price, you should instantly add 10 percent to the price you are shown. Such a price is the true value.

If you don't want to undersell your home, don't let agents compare your home with homes that have been undersold.

CONTROL WAY 10
CONTROL UNDERSELLING

Every agent witnesses homes being undersold. It goes on all the time. Especially at auctions where agents see buyers pay less than they are willing to pay.

Here's another common happening in real estate: One salesperson will get an offer on a home while, at the same time, another salesperson obtains a higher offer. The agents never tell the sellers about the second (higher) offer. This is because the lower offer is with the salesperson who listed the home or the manager/owner of the agency.

Ask an agent: *"Do you see many instances of homes being undersold? Be honest now."*

Let the agent know that you know most homes are undersold.

Not with you, not on this home.

CONTROLLING YOUR PRICE

The problem for sellers is not that buyers won't pay more for homes, it's that most agents can't persuade buyers to offer more. Or, just as often, they can't be bothered.

In addition to the 42 Rules of Negotiation (available to download at jenman.com.au), here are five powerful methods that can help increase the price of your home.

LOVE OR MONEY: Merely asking buyers: *"What's more important, your money or your happiness?"* can make buyers offer a higher price, especially for a home they love.

REGRET HURTS: *"You love this home, so if you refuse to pay the sellers' price, you'll likely regret it for years. If you buy a cheaper home that you don't love, you'll always feel sad knowing you should have bought the home that won your heart."*

> What's more important, your money or your happiness?

THE EGO BUSTER: This is tough, but it often works. If buyers offer you a low price, discreetly suggest they can't afford your home. They should try a cheaper area rather than trying to get you to sell for the price in cheaper areas. You'll be amazed how often the ego kicks in – and they pay your price.

LIFE'S TOO SHORT: As an agent, I would often (gently) say to buyers: *"When you die, do you think you'll have at least a hundred thousand dollars?"* They'd say yes. I'd then say, *"So why not use that money now and buy the home you love? Life is too short not to enjoy."*

AGENT TEST: Tell the agent: *"This is where you should earn that big commission. Let's see how good you are. Go and negotiate the right price for us."*

CONTROL WAY 11
CONTROL THE VPA SCAM

"Always look for the truth from the ground up,
rarely from the top down."

John Pilger 9/10/39–30/12/23

VPA is a rip-off. It's the most common scam in the real estate world, a true Australian rort.

VPA stands for
VENDOR PAID ADVERTISING.

Home sellers are coerced into wasting thousands of dollars on needless advertising for the most misleading of reasons.

The crucial point to understand about VPA is:

Advertising is not done to promote homes for sale.
Advertising is done to promote agents.

Agents call it "building profile".

Surely you have noticed the billboards in your area. Agents' faces at bus stops. Office windows once filled with homes are now filled with mugshots of agents.

In their obsession to appear respectable, these egocentric agents look stupid.

But stupidity is a common characteristic in real estate. And there are few better examples of egotism mixed with stupidity than the self-promotion of agents. As Somerset Maugham wrote, *"Respectability is the cloak under which fools cover their stupidity."*

Do you look at photographs of agents – some unshaven and unkempt – and think, *"Oh, how gorgeous, we must list our home with this agent."*

CAPTION: *This agent seems to think motorcycle skills help home sellers. Let's hope sellers also test his negotiation skills.*

If agents want to pump up their own egos, you should not pay for their narcissism.

Australia is the only country[33] where agents persuade sellers to pay for advertising costs in advance of their homes being sold. In all other countries, any costs of selling a home are included in the commission. If homes don't sell, it's the agents not the sellers who take the risks and pay the costs. That's because the rewards – in huge commissions – are so large.

As one savvy home seller described what happens in real estate in Australia:

"Agents try to place the risks on to their clients." [34]

Here are some truths about typical real estate advertising – especially VPA:

WHY USE AN AGENT?

As mentioned, if advertising is the reason your home sells, why use an agent? Why not place your own advertisement and save tens of thousands of dollars in commission and needless costs?

AGENTS ALREADY HAVE BUYERS!

The reason sellers go to agents is because they expect agents to have buyers. Just as when you go to a butcher, you expect meat. Imagine if you walked into a butcher to order some steaks and the butcher said, *"Give me your money to advertise to find cows!"*

BUY A BUYER

You go to a real estate agent because, effectively, you want to "buy a buyer"; you do NOT go to an agent to buy advertising to promote the agent.

Agents have buyers on their books. If not, they often get many buyers enquiring about the one house, so if they keep records, they will have plenty of leftover buyers.

DID THE AGENT JUST OPEN FOR BUSINESS?

If the first thing an agent does is ask you for money to find buyers, you need to immediately hit back and say: *"Oh, I thought you had been in business for years. I didn't realise you have just opened your business and you don't have any buyers."*

BEING UNETHICAL IS COMPULSORY

Many agents – especially networks – have a shamelessly dishonest policy of charging every seller thousands of dollars for needless advertising. This charge is levied on sellers whether they need it or not. The sellers' needs are secondary. Agents always have a need to promote themselves especially with OPM.[35] "Money for nothing", as Mark Knopfler wrote.

SHEER LAZINESS

If you fund an expensive marketing campaign, you will fund the laziness of an agent.

Everything will revolve around advertisements for your home. If you don't get much response, the agent will give you "bad news", saying: *"We are not getting much enquiry."*

You will then be asked to pay more money for more advertising.

A great truth of advertising is this:

"Advertising is what salespeople do when they are too lazy to follow up prospects." [36]

If your agent is lazy, you will be asked to reward that laziness and give the agent more of an excuse to be lazy.

Tell the agent you have an idea: Instead of using your money to find buyers, the agent can use another method: WORK.

IT NEEDS WORK TO FIND BUYERS

Back in the old days – when agents were respected (rather than despised) – they used to act differently. The first thing agents did when they listed a home was think: *"Who do I know who would be interested in buying this home?"*

If they couldn't recall someone from memory, they would comb their "buyer contacts". They'd call prospective buyers about the home they just listed. They would set appointments – at times that suited buyers (not agents) – to show the home.

At the very least, agents should contact the buyers on their books before they even think of advertising your home – or, worse, asking you to pay for advertising.

Here's how to control the agents and ensure they work instead of asking for your money.

Before you sign up with the agent, ask:

"Do you have any buyers who may like this property?"

Every agent will certainly say, "Yes". Of course, they have interested buyers.

You should then look puzzled – if you know the TV detective *Columbo*,[37] you'll understand how to act – and you'll now ask:

"Why ask us for advertising money to find buyers when you already know buyers? Shouldn't you contact those buyers before asking me for money, which, as I'm sure you know, will attract the same buyers?"

Agents should contact the buyers on their books instead of coercing sellers to pay money so that those buyers contact the agents.

Here's a powerful question for agents.

"How often do you advertise a home and you know the buyers who contact you?"

The honest answer is: *"All the time."*

Some agents think it's smart to get sellers to pay thousands of dollars in advertising money (to promote the agents). It's not smart. It's unethical.

It's also likely illegal – even fraudulent – to tell sellers you need money to advertise their homes when you already have buyers.

THINK "HARDWARE STORE"

Before 2000, when owners sold, their first stop was often a hardware store not an agent.

The owners would get a dozen keys cut. They'd drop off one key at each real estate office and say:

"The first agent to get the best price for my home gets the commission."

Way back (pre-1980s), there were no "Listing Agreements". No signing up home sellers. No legal obligation on sellers. No risk of being sued by agents. Everything was done by handshake. The agent who sold the house got paid. Agents who didn't sell it, didn't get paid.

Those were the days of "OPEN LISTINGS" also known as "GENERAL LISTINGS".

As recently as the early 1990s, most listings in most areas (especially Queensland) were OPEN LISTINGS.

Open listings still exist today – although many agents refuse them. Agents want to be sure that if they do any work, they get paid. Open listings give agents no control.

Some sellers still persuade agents to work on an "OPEN LISTING" basis. In summary, they simply say: *"If you have a buyer, bring them to our home. If they make an offer and it's good enough, it may be accepted."*

WARNING: An "OPEN LISTING" is not always in a seller's best interests. It can encourage buyers to buy from the agent who secures the lowest price. Be careful. As with anything, THINK IT OVER.

BUYERS CIRCULATE

Unlike sellers, buyers do not stay with one agent.[38] They circulate among agents. Therefore, buyers known to one agent are known to other agents.

This is why it's important to choose the agent who's the best negotiator.

> "OPEN LISTING" is not always in a seller's best interests.

If you don't already have a copy, download the *42 Rules of Real Estate Negotiation* at jenman.com.au. This 28-page booklet can help you select an agent who's a good negotiator.

BEWARE THE "NUMBERS" MYTHS

When you consider how many sales are made in a suburb each month,[39] you'll understand how agents use the myth of "numbers" to control sellers. You will also understand the absurdity of what most agents sprout – and most sellers believe – about marketing. Agents will bombard you about "attracting more buyers". All false promises based on the "more buyers" myth. Yet thousands of sellers are seduced. They believe the myths.

Here's a mix of myths on attracting "more buyers"...

- ✓ You'll get more buyers if you use me.
- ✓ You'll have access to 16,000 buyers on my database.
- ✓ You'll get more buyers with our tailored marketing.
- ✓ Our national network attracts buyers across Australia.
- ✓ Our Asian agents attract more Asian buyers.
- ✓ Our Arabic agents attract more Middle Eastern buyers.
- ✓ Our open inspections attract more buyers.
- ✓ Our auctions attract many surplus buyers.
- ✓ Our large team all have more buyers.
- ✓ Our signage in the area attracts more buyers.
- ✓ Our positive reviews attract more buyers.
- ✓ Our print media attracts more buyers.
- ✓ Our commitment to use all major websites attracts more buyers.
- ✓ Our contact with local business attracts more buyers.
- ✓ Our association with lenders and brokers attracts more buyers.
- ✓ Our low quoting of your home's price attracts more buyers.

  Many of these myths are brutally effective at controlling naïve prospective sellers.

  But here's a fact no agent will tell you …

- ✓ Our conditioning with rubbish about "numbers of buyers" means we condition you to accept a lower price. You didn't think using "top agent" meant top price, did you?

And here's an obvious question...

HOW MANY BUYERS DO YOU NEED?

Of course, you only need one buyer – the one who pays you the best price.

Those were the days of "OPEN LISTINGS" also known as "GENERAL LISTINGS".

As recently as the early 1990s, most listings in most areas (especially Queensland) were OPEN LISTINGS.

Open listings still exist today – although many agents refuse them. Agents want to be sure that if they do any work, they get paid. Open listings give agents no control.

Some sellers still persuade agents to work on an "OPEN LISTING" basis. In summary, they simply say: *"If you have a buyer, bring them to our home. If they make an offer and it's good enough, it may be accepted."*

WARNING: An "OPEN LISTING" is not always in a seller's best interests. It can encourage buyers to buy from the agent who secures the lowest price. Be careful. As with anything, THINK IT OVER.

BUYERS CIRCULATE

Unlike sellers, buyers do not stay with one agent.[38] They circulate among agents. Therefore, buyers known to one agent are known to other agents.

This is why it's important to choose the agent who's the best negotiator.

> "OPEN LISTING" is not always in a seller's best interests.

If you don't already have a copy, download the *42 Rules of Real Estate Negotiation* at jenman.com.au. This 28-page booklet can help you select an agent who's a good negotiator.

BEWARE THE "NUMBERS" MYTHS

When you consider how many sales are made in a suburb each month,[39] you'll understand how agents use the myth of "numbers" to control sellers. You will also understand the absurdity of what most agents sprout – and most sellers believe – about marketing. Agents will bombard you about "attracting more buyers". All false promises based on the "more buyers" myth. Yet thousands of sellers are seduced. They believe the myths.

Here's a mix of myths on attracting "more buyers"...

✓ You'll get more buyers if you use me.

✓ You'll have access to 16,000 buyers on my database.

✓ You'll get more buyers with our tailored marketing.

✓ Our national network attracts buyers across Australia.

✓ Our Asian agents attract more Asian buyers.

✓ Our Arabic agents attract more Middle Eastern buyers.

✓ Our open inspections attract more buyers.

✓ Our auctions attract many surplus buyers.

✓ Our large team all have more buyers.

✓ Our signage in the area attracts more buyers.

✓ Our positive reviews attract more buyers.

✓ Our print media attracts more buyers.

✓ Our commitment to use all major websites attracts more buyers.

✓ Our contact with local business attracts more buyers.

✓ Our association with lenders and brokers attracts more buyers.

✓ Our low quoting of your home's price attracts more buyers.

Many of these myths are brutally effective at controlling naïve prospective sellers.

But here's a fact no agent will tell you ...

✓ Our conditioning with rubbish about "numbers of buyers" means we condition you to accept a lower price. You didn't think using "top agent" meant top price, did you?

And here's an obvious question...

HOW MANY BUYERS DO YOU NEED?

Of course, you only need one buyer – the one who pays you the best price.

Now, considering there are only a certain number of sales in your area each month, don't you think it would be smarter to...

NARROW YOUR FOCUS ON TO FINDING THAT ONE RIGHT BUYER

rather than paying thousands of dollars to reach millions of non-buyers?

Even the most junior marketing student knows that one of the biggest mistakes in marketing is to pay to reach people who will never buy your product.

Australia's biggest property website boasts 1.7 million visitors daily.[40] The attitude has developed that "you *must* advertise on this site". Their rates increase constantly. But the costs are paid by sellers – all of whom are naïve, misled and misinformed under the VPA (Vendor Paid Advertising) system.

Add in other websites[41] that agents use – and suddenly the agent who's pitching for your business (and claims to be a "marketing expert") says "you can reach 2 million buyers every day". That's 14 million buyers each week.

That's a lot of NUMBERS.

But it's a trap.

Imagine what happens in two or three weeks IF a home does not sell? The agent then has a powerful argument for persuading the sellers to lower their price.

The advertising control pitch is simple: *"Hundreds of thousands of people have seen your home (online) and it hasn't sold. Therefore, you should drop your price. Listen to the market. Sure, I may have quoted you more before you listed, but I always said we would 'see the market's response'. Well, the market has spoken, and you need to listen. If not, your price may get worse."*

BIG POINT: Many sellers resist lowering their price to "meet the market". These sellers know they are being manipulated. They find better agents and get a better price. Sometimes hundreds of thousands of dollars more – in the same market conditions. The market plays a part, sure. But the biggest part is played by the knowledge and skill of the agent.

Better agents get better prices.

Let's do some maths on those massive advertising numbers:

You are paying to reach approximately 2 million "buyers" a day.

Better agents get better prices.

Your one buyer that you need may or may not be among those 2 million.

Or, in 7 days, you have reached 14 million buyers. Let's call them "lookers" – as we are about to see how many are *NOT BUYERS for your home.*

There are 10,000 residential sales in Australia each week.

So, of those 14 million lookers, 13,990,000 do not buy a home.

Consider the number of sales in your area each week – say a dozen (or you choose).

That's *about...*

TWO GENUINE BUYERS PER DAY
who buy in your area.

Whatever the number for your area, it's a long way from the two million you pay to reach.[42]

You are being coerced (conned) into marketing to TWO MILLION TIME WASTERS per day.

Buyers interested in your area are the only ones of interest to you.

There are 3,330 postcodes in Australia.

Millions of real estate lookers are from those postcodes.

As just seen, 1,999,998 are NOT buyers in your area.

And yet, if an agent tells you to pay thousands of dollars for marketing, *you'll pay to reach people who do not want your home.*

So, why are you chasing thousands of lookers
who'll never buy in
your area??

It makes no sense.

UNLESS...

Unless there are other reasons.

Unless you are being financially used and abused.

A reminder...

THREE REASONS AGENTS ADVERTISE

<u>Reason One</u>: To **PROMOTE AGENTS** AND REAL ESTATE NETWORKS.

If agents really wanted to find a buyer for your home, they would do a lot better than making you pay to advertise to hundreds of thousands of lookers who will never buy your home.

<u>THINK ABOUT THIS:</u> In marketing, it's stupid to advertise to people who cannot buy your product. If you sold surfboards, you wouldn't advertise in nursing homes.

<u>Reason Two</u>: To **CONTROL AND CONDITION SELLERS.**

Without advertising, agents would lose one of their best control strategies. It's common for agents to say: *"How can we get sellers to drop their price if we don't advertise?!"*

> It's stupid to advertise to people who cannot buy your product.

And get this: When a good agent explains the truth – and the dangers – of advertising, especially excessive advertising, other agents will typically tell sellers that the reason their home hasn't sold is because it has "not been marketed correctly". Sellers constantly fall for this trick, change agents, and spend thousands of dollars on marketing to no effect.

IMPORTANT POINT: One of the main reasons agents persuade sellers to pay for the cost of advertising is because they know it doesn't work. They are not going to waste thousands of dollars of their own money on needless marketing.

No, after profile building, the reason for advertising is to control sellers.

And get this: If you agree to pay for a costly marketing campaign, you are literally:

Paying to control and condition yourself!

Do not fall for the "NUMBERS TRAP". The only number you are interested in attracting is...

THE ONE RIGHT BUYER.

So, narrow your focus and use the laser approach not the blunderbuss approach and make sure that all those who want to "look" at your home are qualified and identified.

Reason Three: To **FIND NEW LEADS** FOR THE AGENTS.

What's the question typical agents ask when they receive any enquiry on a listing?

"Do you have a property to sell?"

Because many buyers also intend to sell a property, often in the same area, advertising is how agents find such new listing leads. At the expense of the sellers.

Here is one of the most persuasive yet deceptive statements agents make to sellers:

"It's your home, it's only fair you pay for advertising."

This statement makes sellers – especially fair and decent ones – feel inclined to pay up. But if you want to control the agent instead of the agent controlling you, here's what to say:

"We understand your point about being 'fair'. So, we will pay for the cost of marketing our home if we own the leads that come from the advertising we pay for."

The agent will do a double-take. Some may pretend not to understand. So, you can say:

"If you find other sellers from the advertising we pay for – and you sell their homes – who gets the commission from those sales? Do you give us those commissions, or do you keep them?"

Here's the reality: The agent wants you to pay for advertising that creates more commission, but the agent wants to keep the commission.

What kind of a business deal is that? The person who puts up 100% of the cost gets nothing – and the person who puts up nothing gets 100% of the profit?

The VPA system is a scam. Don't fall for it. Don't pay anything before you sell.

THE UP-SELL TRICK

Be aware of another scam that goes with VPA.

Agents will say you need to be "seen by more buyers" so you need to pay extra (thousands of dollars) to have your home featured at the top when buyers look for homes in your area. They will say you must have a "Premium" online ad.

You think you'll get priority – an advantage not available to most sellers. That's what the agent wants you to think.

But guess what?

Everyone is told the same – "Pay extra for a 'premium' ad and your home will be the first one buyers see."

> How can every home be the first that buyers see?

But how can every home be the first that buyers see?

The "Up-sell Trick" is one of the most common scams in real estate. Sellers across Australia are conned out of thousands of dollars each – hundreds of millions of dollars collectively – by agents clamouring to increase their "profile" at the expense of naïve and trusting sellers.

BEWARE: Owners who realise the "Premium" scam too late, and refuse to pay, usually find themselves sued by agents or their minions. When they express their outrage, they will be told to *"Read the Listing Agreement you signed"*.

If they try to lodge a negative review on Rate-My-Agent, they discover that only successful sellers can leave reviews.

INSIDE STORY: On 1 September 2019, I flew from Brisbane to Melbourne.[43] I sat beside an executive from a large real estate website.[44] This person admitted that "Premium Ad" campaigns are misleading. She said: *"When I sold my home,[45] the agent asked me to pay $6,000 for advertising.[46] I told him to get f---ed. I said I worked for a real estate website and that a small hundred-dollar ad is more effective than an ad costing thousands of dollars."* [47]

This executive said: "I know that the smallest ads have the same – or greater response – than the larger ads."[48]

It gets worse.

The website companies offer "special deals" to agents:

"If you guarantee that ALL your sellers will be 'upsold' to a Premium ad, we'll give YOU a huge discount."

This discount is rarely passed on to sellers.

Many agents charge sellers the standard rate for a Premium ad and pocket the difference between the standard rate and the discount.

When selling your home, reject Premium advertising.

REAL BUYERS ALWAYS FIND HOMES

Homebuyers are a resourceful lot.

They can spend hours, days, weeks, even months searching for a home.

Buyers do not visit a website and stop once they view the "Premium" ads; indeed, many buyers skip the more expensive ads.

Buyers love to feel that they have found a great home – not a home most buyers have rejected.

Real estate websites have personal parameters and settings. Buyers enter their requirements, and the website reveals homes that are a "match" regardless of how much sellers have spent advertising their homes.

The right buyers will find your home without you wasting thousands of dollars on needless advertising.

According to an executive at Australia's biggest real estate website, the highest selling agent in the city of Melbourne[49] spends the least amount of money advertising on their website.[50]

YOU CAN SELL A SECRET

Another common line used by agents to control sellers and ensure they spend big on advertising is: "You can't sell a secret."

But of course you *can* sell a secret.

And, as any skilled negotiator knows, a "secret" often sells for a much higher price than a similar product that's flogged on the massmarket.

Many buyers are acutely conscious of privacy. To some, it's a major requirement.

They don't want homes that thousands of sticky-beaks, neighbours and deplorables have traipsed through. They don't want interior photographs and floor plans displayed online for years after the sale.

Privacy is a big selling point.

Privacy is a big selling point.

So is security. Safety is paramount to many buyers, especially the most well-heeled.

If you remove these two benefits from your home, you'll lose some of the best paying buyers, without whom you may have to sell for hundreds of thousands of dollars less.

Even millions of dollars less.

This is especially true in high-end homes which attract high-net-worth people and celebrities, most of whom rank privacy and security as essential buying requirements.

To the alarm of real estate networks and websites – who regularly release misleading propaganda to support their fallacious arguments – well-informed sellers are now demanding that their homes be sold without specific mass marketing.

These switched-on sellers are turning the tables on the agents.

These sellers now control the agents by stressing the benefits of not advertising, which can clearly outweigh any benefits of advertising.

Indeed, while advertising is hugely beneficial for agents, the benefits, if any, for sellers, are all outweighed by the disadvantages to sellers.

Smart sellers are now discovering that one of the best ways to get the best price for their homes – and, at the same time, control the selling process – is to demand what's called:

AN OFF-MARKET SALE

An off-market sale does not mean your home is not on the market; it means you get a better price because you hire a smart and ethical agent who knows how to find the best buyer for your home without throwing your home in among the mass-controlled sellers.

An off-market sale stops the stupidity and dishonesty of agents controlling sellers by forcing them to spend thousands of dollars marketing their home to millions of non-buyers.

Always remember: While millions of lookers will not buy your home and therefore be of no benefit to you, these lookers are of huge benefit to the industry. Agents promote themselves to millions of people at your expense. No wonder agents love VPA; it costs them nothing.

Since the VPA system was introduced in the late 1980s, it has, over the ensuing years, spread across the nation as more agents abandoned ethical behaviour in favour of self-interest.

Today, at least 90 percent of agents use the VPA scam to control sellers.

Like the prickly pear plague that decimated the income of farmers in the 1920s, the VPA plague decimates the income of home sellers in the 2020s.

The only sellers who can now avoid being hurt by VPA are those who refuse to be controlled.

As more sellers learn to resist the cliches of agents, more agents are accepting a fact of survival for them: *If they want to list your home, they must do so under your terms.*

You must have control, not the agent. An off-market sale gives sellers wonderful control.

So successful is the off-market method of selling that many industry players are now seriously alarmed, even terrified. These big influencers can read the play. They can see homes being sold for higher prices with less or no advertising – and they don't like it. Consequently, they are doing what they always do – the stupid response not the smart response.

The stupid response is to increase the sophistry to prevent sellers rejecting VPA or off-market sales. More articles planted in the media (who own the major websites), urging sellers to spend more money on advertising. Even warning them against off-market selling.

The smart response – which many agents are now choosing – is to embrace a method that's best for the sellers. Off-market selling and rejecting VPA is best for sellers.

If you follow the control suggestions in this book, you *will* find an agent who *will* agree to an off-market sale without using the VPA scam on you.

HOW SECRETS SUCCEED

*A perfect example of how home sellers can sell
for thousands of dollars more
by keeping control rather than surrendering
control to the agents (like most sellers).*

In 2023, a couple wanted to buy a second home in a favoured location in a regional city.

They had two major requirements: A lovely home and one not flogged to the market. Privacy and security were essential requirements. They refused to inspect homes that were mass-advertised or open for public inspection.

They made it clear to several agents that if a home became available in their favoured location, they were willing to pay above-market value. But only for an off-market sale.

Within two weeks an agent called: He had just listed a lovely home.

The buyers were the first (and only) buyers to inspect this home.

The agent said the home would soon come on the market at between $900,000 and $1 million.

The buyers knew its true value was probably between $800,000 and $900,000.

Nevertheless, the home was perfect for them. Exactly what they wanted.

They asked the agent: *"What price will we have to pay so the owners will sell to us today?"*

The agent said he would contact the owners and ask that question.

The buyers waited nervously. The longer they waited, the more they desired the home – and the more they told themselves they were willing to pay. Fortunately, they were affluent. The home and their privacy were far more important to them than the price of the home.

A few hours later, the agent called the buyers. His tone indicated he had bad news. He said, *"I spoke to the owners. If you want to buy this home today, you'll have to pay $1,125,000."*

This price was as much as $325,000 above the home's true value. Even if it had sold for $1 million on the open market, the buyers were still being asked to pay $125,000 above its value.

The buyers didn't hesitate. They said yes, they'll take it.[51]

The moral of this true story is clear: Despite what some agents say, you *can* sell a secret. If you have the right home that suits the right buyer, you *can* sell a secret for hundreds of thousands of dollars above its value on the open mass market.[52]

DON'T DAMAGE THE VALUE

Advertising can damage the value of your home, especially online advertising where prospects track the number of "views". If your home does not sell in a few weeks, it's stale. This causes low offers. No matter how low the price, the agent still wants a big commission.

As just mentioned, the right buyers often pay extra for a home that has never been advertised.

It's counter intuitive: The less you advertise, the more you protect your value.

RELY ON "PULLER" ADS

Ask most agents, *"How many of your listings are advertised?"* Most will say, *"All of them."* This reveals their stupidity and lack of basic marketing knowledge. Or, more accurately, it once again proves that the real purpose of advertising is to control sellers – not find buyers.

> The less you advertise, the more you protect your value.

Agents do not have to advertise every listing to attract every buyer. They only need to advertise a handful of "attracting" homes. This attracts plenty of enquiry. These homes become their "puller ads", enabling the agent to offer homes not advertised. This solves the problem of damaging the value of homes.

The only disadvantage is that agents lose one of their main conditioning tools. But that's not your problem. Your problem is to protect the value of your home and still have the same – or an even better – chance of selling for the best price.

IDEA: Rather than wasting thousands of dollars on needless advertising, there are better things agents can do to attract qualified buyers. Like working – following up buyers rather than waiting for buyers to contact them.

Also, agents could **OPEN THEIR DOORS** on weekends and after hours (say, until 7 pm) when buyers are most available.

The best-paying buyers (family-home buyers not investors) visit an area before they buy. Most buyers are most available after 5 pm and weekends. That's when most agents close. It makes no sense. A Golden Rule of selling is: *"Make it easy for buyers to buy."* Most agents make it hard for buyers. Just speak with any buyers to discover their frustration.

Whatever you do...

NEVER HIRE A LAZY AGENT.[53]

CONTROL WAY 12
THE MAGIC OF ENTHUSIASM

Selling is often called the "transference of enthusiasm". The more an agent likes your home, the more chance you will get a better result.

If an agent appeals to you, give them a tour of your property. Gauge their interest. Show them all the features and benefits that will interest prospective buyers.

It is important to have an agent who shows enthusiasm for your home. If the agent shows little interest in your home (other than how much you want), do not hire that agent.

Later, when you are listed, "MYSTERY SHOP" the agent. Ask a friend to enquire about your home. The agent should know

> The more an agent likes your home, the more chance you will get a better result.

that you will monitor their service if you hire them. Make sure they are okay with this. How could they object without appearing dodgy?

Having agents know that you will be checking up on them is one of the best ways to control their behaviour once they list your home.

Remember the saying: *"What gets inspected, gets respected."*

CONTROL WAY 13
PREPARE A LOVE LIST

Once your home is for sale, you'll have enough fault-finding by buyers or agents trying to control you. Control these negatives by preparing a positive list of your home's best features.

So, grab a sheet of quality paper and prepare your "Love List". Use the heading: **WHY WE LOVE OUR HOME** – and let the good points pour out of you.

You should be able to list 50 points you love about your home. Some owners list 100+.

And then, every time any buyer shows the slightest interest, be sure the agent gives them your "Love List". *"The owners thought you may like to know some reasons they love this home."*

And remember, you are never "anxious" or worse, "desperate" to sell. The right words to use are that you are "reluctantly selling your much-loved home". If it's true, of course.

Agents may bombard you with what buyers dislike about your home. This is just another attempt to control you and persuade you to lower your price. But when you hit back with your Love List, you keep control. You are persuading buyers to increase their price. And for agents to remember all the positive points of your home. You'll love the power of your Love List.

CONTROL WAY 14
STRIVE TO FIND A "HEART BUYER"

There are two "types" of property buyers: Investors and family-home buyers.

Investors focus on dollars. Most want to buy cheaply. Some investors make extremely low offers on many properties hoping one desperate (naïve) seller will accept. Some learn this technique at "get rich seminars" where a self-titled "property millionaire" milks the wanna-be millionaires with such ideas as: *"Inspect 50 properties and offer low prices on every one of them. Don't be scared to go too low. Even offer half-price. If one says yes, you are on your way to being rich."* Always ignore ridiculously low or obviously insulting offers.

You will get a better price from family-home buyers. To these buyers, price is not as important as love. If buyers love your home, they will pay a premium price. Win their hearts and you'll win a higher price.

When buyers love a home, they strive to own it. They sell assets. They enlist support from relatives. They increase borrowings. All because your home has won their heart.

As a famous saying goes: *"The heart has reasons that reason itself knows nothing about."*[54]

If more agents focused on love before price, more sellers would get better prices.

Tell your agent you are hoping to find a HEART BUYER.

> **WARNING:** As mentioned, don't be stubborn. If a heart buyer appears, it may be in the first few days – even hours – of your home being for sale. If not, accept that your goal must be to get the highest price – not an impossible-to-achieve price.
>
> As an agent, I joked with stubborn sellers by saying: *"At this price, the buyers for your home have yet to be conceived."*
>
> **IMPORTANT TIP:** Many sellers make the mistake of demanding too much for their homes and then, when they buy another home, paying too much. You should look at your entire property transaction – selling and buying again – as one major financial event, not two.
>
> Put as much effort into buying for a lower price as you do into selling for a higher price.

CONTROL WAY 15
CHECK YOUR NEIGHBOURS

So often in life we overlook the obvious.

Many sellers spend thousands of dollars on marketing only to have their home bought by their next-door neighbour.

The first people who should be approached about the sale of your home are neighbours; indeed, everyone in your street. Or, better still, every homeowner in your block.

> So often in life we overlook the obvious.

Residents like the local area. Some have friends or relatives keen to buy locally. This idea can yield a great result, especially if you live in a "tightly held" location.

Why commit to thousands of dollars in advertising, ostensibly to find a buyer, if the right buyer lives next door?!

Be sure to stress this (control) point to all agents. If they are not prepared to approach your nearby neighbours (at least), do not select them as your agent.

At Jenman Support, we often help sellers approach local residents before hiring an agent. We design a flyer with a brief message stating that a home will soon be for sale and, if anyone wants to inspect prior to listing, to contact the owner direct.

This can save sellers thousands of dollars in advertising costs, plus tens of thousands of dollars in commission.

OFFER: In return for purchasing this book, we can help you design a simple flyer to send to nearby homeowners in your area.

Just email support@jenman.com.au or call 1800 1800 18.

CONTROL WAY 16
INSIST ON "SOLE AGENCY"
REFUSE EXCLUSIVE AGENCY

When sellers sign an "Exclusive Agency Agreement" they surrender control to the agent.

Exclusive Agency means you *EXCLUDE YOURSELF.* You lose the right to sell your own home. Even if the agent does nothing, the agent still gets paid.

To keep control, **INSIST ON A SOLE AGENCY AGREEMENT** not an Exclusive Agency Agreement. This gives you the right to sell your home yourself without paying commission.

If you trust yourself more than you trust an agent, if you want control of the sale process, be sure you reject an Exclusive Agency and only sign a Sole Agency.

Sure, if the agent has done some work – or if the agent helps you negotiate with a buyer sourced by you – you may pay some commission. At your discretion.

The important point, however, is this:

A SOLE AGENCY GIVES THE SELLERS CONTROL
– NOT THE AGENTS.

SOLE AGENCY AGREEMENT
Particulars of Appointment
AGENT
  SCOTT KIM REAL ESTATE
  PTY LTD
  5 Barlyn Road, Mount
  Waverley Vic 3149
  Tel: (03) 9808 0481
  sales@scottkim.com.au
  www.scottkim.com.au

EXCLUSIVE SALE AUTHORITY
Particulars of Appointment
AGENT DETAILS
  Agent:
  Address:
  Attention:
  Phone:
  Email:

CONTROL WAY 17
ALWAYS CITE "HIGHER AUTHORITY"

Let's be clear about a vital point: When any salesperson (from any industry) urges you to sign something, it's mostly for their benefit. Agents are trained to persuade you to sign their exclusive agreement as soon as possible with as little thought as possible.

When this happens, they have "GOT YA".

Always do something that agents try to stop you doing – **THINK ABOUT IT.**

Make it your family policy – just as agents make a "company policy" – that you...

DON'T SIGN ANYTHING!

without reading it thoroughly, thinking about it carefully and,
finally, getting independent legal or professional advice
(from someone who's focused on your best interests).

In the *42 Rules of Modern Real Estate Negotiation*
(download at jenman.com.au),

Rule 37 is the **HIGHER AUTHORITY RULE.** It states...

This rule is best used when you want to extricate yourself from a position where you are under intense stress, such as when someone is using high pressure to get your sellers to make a decision that they don't feel comfortable making. In that situation, you just say that they cannot make a final decision until you speak to "another person" – this "Higher Authority".

Neil's higher authority as a young man; his adopted father, Alec Shev.

CONTROL WAY 18
42 WAYS TO A BETTER RESULT

In 2015, after years of research, I wrote a course called *The Real Estate Negotiation Course.*

It was written for agents to show them how to negotiate the best price for sellers.

Included in the course was the: 42 Rules of Modern Real Estate Negotiation in a 28-page booklet.

Just as doctors know the 206 bones in a body, agents should know the 42 Rules of Negotiation.

Each rule can help homeowners get a better price.

I suggested to real estate managers that all their agents should learn, by heart, the 42 Rules. Most couldn't be bothered.

In 2020, I decided to make the 42 Rules available to sellers as well as agents; however, if you meet an agent who can recite and explain the 42 Rules, seriously consider hiring them.[55]

Available to download at jenman.com.au

CONTROL WAY 19
A SENSIBLE INSPECTION SYSTEM

The "open inspection" system is absurd. It's not designed to find buyers. It's one of the major ways agents control sellers. This is one of those "if-only-you-knew" points that make sellers wild when they realise what's happening. It's coercive control.

Agents benefit in three ways with open inspections.

First, agents are **promoting themselves (again).**

Second, agents are **attracting other sellers.** Homeowners who are thinking of selling visit open inspections. Some agents deliberately increase the number of open houses plus they deliberately delay the sale to attract more sellers. In the words of two real estate sales trainers:

Trainer 1: *"The worst thing you can do is sell the house that's open for inspection."* Selling a home stops your source of seller leads from that home.[56]

Trainer 2: *"The mistake some agents make is selling the home at the first open inspection."* Agents maximise the number of open houses to maximise the new sellers they find.[57]

Third, agents use open inspections to **condition sellers.**

While open inspections are good for agents, they are rarely good for sellers – for six reasons.

Reason 1: Inconvenient for buyers. You'd better hope the chosen half-hour each week suits the best buyers. If not, you'll miss out.

Reason 2: Buyers who don't like your home – especially sticky-beaks – often denigrate your home within earshot of other buyers.

Reason 3: As all "lookers" are not qualified, the agent can't easily detect the best prospects.

Reason 4: It's dangerous. Burglars and home-invaders "case" your home.[58]

Reason 5: Your insurance doesn't cover you; visitors (buyers?) are "invited guests".

Reason 6: You lose buyers for whom privacy is paramount.

SOLUTION: All inspections should be by **PRE-APPOINTMENT** with qualified buyers.

Keep control of those who inspect your home.

Refuse to allow your home to be used to raise the "profile" of the agent or as a source of leads.

> All inspections should be by PRE-APPOINTMENT with qualified buyers.

CONTROL WAY 20
ALLOW ACCESS TO OTHER AGENTS

Once you sign up with some agents, you instantly get passed down to some junior.

The agent who signed you up is now looking for the next seller.

This is the first big letdown with most sellers.

Be sure the agent you select is the agent who does most of the work with your home.

With one important exception – allowing other agents to be involved. You need to make sure that agents are happy to share information about your home with other agents – both in their office and in competing offices.

Do not sign up with agents who hog your home like dogs snarling over bones.

In the United States, the first thing agents do when they list a home is place details of that home into the multiple-listing network (MLS). Any of 1,566,354 agents can find a buyer for the home.

In Australia, the first thing most agents do when they list a home is stop other agents going near that home. And then they delegate the home sellers to a junior or a rookie salesperson.

When agents have control of sellers, agents are in charge. They can refuse to allow other agents near your home. This means sellers can miss the best buyers.

And, at the same time, you are placed in the hands of a junior. This is common with self-titled "top agents". **The reason they make many sales is because they have many junior assistants.**

To keep control, sellers must ensure that any agent from anywhere can show their home.

Please note, however: If another agent (other than the one with whom you listed) finds a buyer for your home, make sure the agent who is more skilled in negotiation handles the negotiation.

A big advantage with allowing other agents to show your home is that you increase your chances of finding the best buyer. The disadvantage is that you could fall into the hands of an agent who's a poor negotiator. Don't let that happen.

The biggest advantage of all, however, is that one agent cannot control your home and ensure that he or she gets the maximum commission regardless of the price you receive. When more agents are involved, the listing agent loses a dangerous control strategy.

That's good for you.

CONTROL WAY 21
BE SCEPTICAL OF BIG BRANDS
"Branding only works on cattle."

Book by Jonathan Salem Maskin

Big brand agents are often the worst. The only qualifications needed to join a big brand network are a pulse and the promise to pay the bosses

– like the mob. They rarely reject or expel any agents. Their obsession is looking big because big attracts sellers.

Often, the bigger the brand, the lower the service and the sale price. Australia's largest brands are regularly the most complained about agents.[59]

> **Big brand agents are often the worst.**

If you want to be treated as important, you'll often get better service and a bigger price from a smaller agent – especially family-owned independent agencies. Be sure to call at least one smaller agency. Don't get controlled by the big brand mirage.

CONTROL WAY 22

WELCOME HONEST FEEDBACK

Be careful that in your desire to avoid conditioning, you do not reject honest feedback.

Some sellers attack the agent and accuse them of "conditioning" no matter what they say.

The way to tell the difference between "conditioning" and "honest feedback" is by gauging the substance and specifics of what an agent is telling you.

> **Do not reject honest feedback.**

If you are being conditioned, the agent will be vague, even secretive. For example: *"The buyers think your land is too small."*

When agents are giving you honest feedback, their message will contain both substance and specifics. They will provide evidence to support their feedback.

Therefore, you should ask your agent: *"Is there anything we can do to make the job of selling our home easier for you?"*

Press the agent to be direct with you. Some agents don't want to offend sellers (or be abused) so they may not disclose important facts you should know.

So, be sure you know the difference between calculated conditioning and honest feedback.

Don't be a shoot-the-messenger seller.

CONTROL WAY 23
RECORD THE AGENT

*"People with good intentions make promises.
People with good character keep them."*

Most agents are master manipulators. They tell you one thing then do another thing.

But not if you use this way of controlling them.

*RECORD ALL THE DIALOGUE
BETWEEN YOU AND THE AGENT.*

You don't act like a police officer doing an interrogation. You just want an accurate record of what you all discuss together.

Who could object to such pragmatism?

Some sellers say that recording the agent's presentation is like giving them a truth drug.

You must do it. It's a great habit to develop – not just with agents but with all salespeople.

I record most of my work calls and meetings – especially when supporting consumers. I often send a copy to them – or their close friends or family.

Having an audio file is not only a perfect record. It's liberating. If anything goes wrong – or if there is an honest misunderstanding – you refer to the audio.

Don't be nervous. Just say:

"The sale of our home is important, and we have people supporting us, so we'd like them to hear what is said. To lessen the chance of any mistakes later, we'll record our chat now."

And then go to your phone, switch on flight mode (to stop interruptions) and start recording.

Honest agents won't mind being recorded. Dishonest agents will say they are "not comfortable". In such cases, I ask: *"Are you ashamed of words that come from your mouth?"*

Make it clear that you are not *asking* to record them, you are disclosing (as the law requires) that you will record them. If they don't like it, they can leave – or end the call if you are recording over the phone. To be sure, you are both being recorded.

A recording gives you wonderful control and a better result.

Agents are less inclined to break their word when they know there is a recording of their words.

CONTROL WAY 24
CONSIDER A FOREIGN AGENT

"Familiarity breeds contempt; distance brings respect."

African proverb

So many local agents are fixated on one factor – price. They make no allowance for the beauty of a home or the benefits of their area.

These agents are PRICE-PREJUDICED.

Often, all agents in an area can suffer from price-prejudice.

This is why owners can get frustrated with local agents; none seem to appreciate that their home is special and valued higher.

Agents will make comments such as: *"Nothing in this area has ever sold above [insert price]"*, thereby confirming that, in their minds, if something has never been done in the past, it can never be done in the future.

That logic would have prevented the invention of the wheel.

> **These agents are PRICE-PREJUDICED.**

SOLUTION: Many times, especially with the most beautiful homes, homeowners can do much better by employing an agent outside their local area. Such "foreign agents" (as they are dubbed) may have a better appreciation of an area than local agents. Outside agents can see what local agents often can't (or won't) see.

So, if you are disappointed in the response from local agents, try meeting a "foreign agent".

> Sally[60] had her home for sale in a small regional area.
> There was only one agent in the area.
> So, naturally, she listed her home with the local agent.
> After a year, the best offer
> the local agent obtained was $312,000.
> Sally decided to use a "foreign agent".
> Within a few weeks, her home was sold – for
> **$550,000.**

CONTROL WAY 25
TAKE YOUR TIME

*"I can give you a six-word formula for success:
Think things through, then follow through."*

Eddie Rickenbacker

It takes years to own your home. First, saving the deposit, then getting finance, then finding the right home, then the costs of buying, followed by years of mortgage payments and maintenance.

All these costs are usually paid from hard-earned wages. So, be careful.

Do not make your greatest-ever cost be the amount you undersell your property. Take the time to do your research and think things over – carefully.

Selling your home may be your biggest financial decision. And yet, many home sellers lose more money selling their home than they earn in two years of wages.

Imagine working two years for nothing. Well, that's the financial equivalent of what can happen if you choose the wrong agent or wrong method of sale. I've seen losses (in terms of amounts properties have undersold) of millions of dollars. Farmers often lose more money from underselling than from profit in all their years farming. This is no exaggeration.

Almost everyone who sells a home (if they bought many years ago) enjoys capital gain. This makes them happy, but it can also make them overlook how much more they should have obtained.

What do you want – a high price or the highest price? The difference can be hundreds of thousands of dollars. And yes, as just mentioned, sometimes millions of dollars.

You cannot be too prudent. It's better to spend two or three weeks looking for the right agent and doing realistic research (not accepting agents' sales pitches) than years wishing you'd given more time and thought to such a major decision.

I've seen elderly people spend the last years of their lives feeling miserable at how much they undersold their family home. And, of course, relatives are shattered to see how much was lost – all because elderly and inexperienced sellers did everything an agent told them. They lost control, which meant they lost massive amounts of money by underselling their property.

So, tell each agent that you need time to consider the options facing you.

Don't be rushed. Control the agents by insisting that you take your time. Hasten slowly.

CONTROL WAY 26
THE ONLY PROMISE YOU SEEK

"Never believe promises from those who lack discipline. They have broken a thousand promises to themselves, and they will break their promises to you."

Matthew Kelly

There is only one promise a good agent can honestly give you – and be confident of keeping:

TO SELL YOUR HOME FOR THE HIGHEST PRICE.

If that price makes you happy
and lets you move on with your life, sell.

If not, stay.

If the agent has worked hard, been honest and achieved the highest price and you decide to stay rather than sell, at least credit the agent with doing their best. If you have been fortunate enough to find a risk-free agent, you'll lose nothing. The agent will have spent their time and their money in achieving the best result for you. Say thanks.

Don't make the mistake of thinking another agent will get you a better price. If the best agent can't get the price you want, the second-best agent will not get a better price.

As mentioned under the topic "Stubborn Sellers", some sellers use a good agent to try and get a great price. If that price cannot be obtained, the sellers go to a typical agent, pay thousands of dollars in needless expenses, and sell for less than the first agent could have obtained.

It's not only rude and unfair, but also stupid.

If the best agent does the best and gets you the best market price, how can you expect more?

The best price is the only promise you should seek. To be sure, it's a great promise and especially rewarding when the agent fulfils it for you.

CONTROL WAY 27
YOUR SUPPORTER OR ADVISER

If you know someone with plenty of genuine successful experience[61] with real estate and you trust that person, enlist their support.

A smart knowledgeable friend can be a great help – not just in getting a better price but in reducing the stress that hits and hurts most sellers.

The old saying *"It's not what you know, it's who you know"* can be so true when it comes to controlling the selling price of your home.

From finding and choosing the right agent to observing the agent's marketing progress and, finally, to the important negotiation phase, having a supporter can make a world of difference.

Most agents will, eventually, ask sellers if they wish to sell for a lower price. This is because most buyers – even those who love the home – will make offers.

Every buyer loves a bargain.

If the agent says that the buyers will not pay any more – and you feel your home is worth more – a good supporter can come up with some powerfully effective suggestions.

At Jenman Support, for example, we help the sellers, *and* we help the agents.

No matter what your concern, you can always contact us.

Of course, sometimes – depending on demand – we can't always offer full support. But, at the very least, we will give every genuine and courteous seller our best effort – and that could be worth many thousands of dollars extra.

> We will give every genuine and courteous seller our best effort – and that could be worth many thousands of dollars extra.

> If you have a trusted real estate expert in your life, enlist their help if you prefer. Do what makes you most comfortable.

Please remember three points with our support service:

Point 1: We never ask you for any money.

Point 2: We never ask you to sign anything.

Point 3: We always fight to protect your best interests.

If you have a trusted real estate expert in your life, enlist their help if you prefer. Do what makes you most comfortable.

If you'd like my support, please email me on support@jenman.com.au. If you are an honest and decent home seller, I will do my best to help you.

PART 4

11 TOP TIPS FOR A TOP RESULT

TOP TIP 1
BE KIND TO BUYERS
DISCLOSE VITAL INFORMATION

"It takes courage to be kind."

Maya Angelou

Real estate is a people business. It's not, as often touted, about "bricks and mortar". It's about feelings and emotions. And worse, near-constant anxiety. If you think selling a home is stressful, try buying a home these days. Most agents treat buyers with disdain, even contempt.

The best buyers for your home will be *people*. They have feelings, fears and emotions that few agents understand or acknowledge. If you treat buyers with care and kindness, that's what you'll get back. It may seem trite, but it's true: You get back what you give out (mostly).

Once you've chosen the best agent and the best method of sale, your most important question is: *"What can we do to WIN the best buyers?"* When your home is for sale, you are not just competing with other homes for sale, you are competing with other home sellers.

Thousands of buyers spend thousands of dollars arranging for building and pest reports on homes they never buy – usually because agents mislead them. Some buyers waste more than ten thousand dollars on inspection reports for homes they don't buy because they got out-bid in a negotiation war or, worse, gazumped. It's frustrating and heartbreaking.

In America, it's largely compulsory for home sellers to disclose this vital information. Due to the corruption in the Australian real estate industry, only the ACT has made it mandatory for home sellers to provide disclosure reports.

Aside from the obvious, like making your entrance welcoming[62] and allowing qualified buyers to see your home at their convenience, try this: Arrange for up-to-date building and pest reports on your home.

It may be a great investment, far better than advertising costs, for sure.

Offer these reports to prospective buyers – at no charge. This will attract more buyers who'll appreciate your consideration and kindness. They'll feel good about you from the start. And then, if they like your home, they'll be more likely to pay their best price.

Buyers like to buy nice homes from nice people; it's good karma. Seriously.

Seneca once said: *"Wherever there is a human, there is an opportunity for kindness."* [63]

If there was only one tip I could give you for getting a better result (price) for your home – and feeling good at the same time – it would be this: Be kind to prospective buyers.

> Be kind to prospective buyers.

TOP TIP 2

THE BEST PAYING BUYERS

Buyers likely to pay the best price have three qualities.

Quality 1. They are FAMILY-HOME buyers.

Quality 2. They LIVE LOCALLY.

Quality 3. They will LOVE your home.

✓ APPEAL. Make sure your home is appealing externally. At least neat and clean.

✓ RENOVATE OR NOT? If your home needs renovating, be careful. Some buyers pay more for unrenovated homes – they can add their personal taste.

> Some buyers pay more for unrenovated homes.

✓ LIKELY PROSPECTS. Think like a detective. WHO will like this home?

For example, if it's near a school, teachers, or parents with children. Use the school noticeboard. If you are near a hospital, target doctors or medical staff.

✓ CONTACT BUYERS ALREADY LOOKING IN YOUR AREA. A good agent will know buyers looking in your area. Before advertising be sure the agent contacts known buyers. And not the lazy way with a group email. A text: *"Good news, we have just listed a lovely home. You are among the first to know. Would you like some details? I think you'll love this."* And then, the agent must follow up by phone. This is called "work". Good agents are go-getters not sit-n-waiters.

✓ DON'T OVER-SELL. A common mistake is too much information before buyers inspect a home. If a buyer is qualified and has the capacity to buy a home and there is a strong chance they'll like the home, the whole aim is: ENTICE AN INSPECTION. Buyers can get more information once they see the home, especially if they are interested. If not, don't give confidential or relevant information to non-buyers.

✓ DON'T NEGOTIATE TOO SOON. Before negotiating the price, if at all, an agent should say: *"Inspect the property first. If you like it, we can discuss price and any other issues later. I think you'll love this home. When can you see it?"*

> Good agents are go-getters not sit-n-waiters.

NEVER NEGOTIATE WITH BUYERS BEFORE THEY INSPECT YOUR HOME.

TOP TIP 3

PROTECT YOUR BOTTOM LINE

"How much last price?"

Common buyer question

Everyone wants to know: *What's your lowest price?*

NEVER REVEAL YOUR LOWEST PRICE.

Revealing their bottom-line price is a trap that catches thousands of home sellers. It causes them to lose massive amounts of money from the sale price.

If you reveal the lowest amount you will accept, that will soon become the highest amount you get.

Ask this obvious question:

Why would anyone want to know the lowest price you will accept?

BEWARE OF AGENTS who, when they meet you, one of their first questions is: *How much do you want?* Or worse: *What's the lowest price you'll accept?*

What business is it of agents (or anyone) the amount of your lowest price?

To protect your bottom line – and achieve the top price for your home – you need two firm goals.

GOAL 1: Keep your lowest price confidential. Never reveal it. Never means never.

GOAL 2. DISCOVER THE HIGHEST PRICE interested buyers are willing to pay.

Whatever you focus upon is what you get.

So, what do you want: A buyer to buy your home at your lowest price or you to sell your home to a buyer for the highest price they are prepared to pay – the BHP?

Negotiate only with buyers who genuinely want your home, not tyre-kickers, lookers, or wanna-be buyers. Unless they are willing to buy, don't negotiate with them.

You or your agent needs to discover their highest price without revealing your lowest price.

This is how you keep control and get the best price.

TOP TIP 4
A 24-HOUR SALESPERSON

A For Sale sign is your 24-hour salesperson.

Buyers can't buy your home unless they know it's for sale. Buyers who are attracted by a For Sale sign are already "sold" on the location. They like your home from the outside and are keen to inspect.

Why would you *not* want to attract such buyers?

Attract the best paying buyers at the lowest marketing cost.

With a sign, you attract the best paying buyers at the lowest marketing cost.

Don't put too much information on a sign. Just enough to pique interest. And never have the agent's face on the sign, unless they pay you – just as they expected you to pay for a sign with their face on it. You are in control now.

Buyers do not buy homes because they like a large photo of an agent.

Buyers buy homes because they like the homes.

When local buyers love a home, they often pay extra. As happens in the bush – as all farmers know – the buyers who pay the most for a farm are often neighbours. Erect a sign and attract the best paying buyers.

NEVER SAY NO TO A FOR SALE SIGN.

Despite the huge benefits, some sellers refuse a For Sale sign. They don't want locals to know their business. But the neighbours will know you're selling once you move, so why not let them know now – and get a better chance of getting a better price?

EXTRA TOP TIP: If you can't find a good agent and you feel your only option is to endure a typical agent, no. *You do have another option.* And it's a beauty.

Get your own sign made. *You will get plenty of calls,* I promise you. Wonderful.

If you're worried about how to handle buyers or negotiate, I will help you – if you're a nice person. Of course, I will. I've helped many lovely people who can't find a good agent, sell without an agent.

And no, I don't want money. Your appreciation is enough reward.

Just call me or my son, Alec, on 1800 1800 18 or text 0427 376 669 or 0477 27 2737.

TOP TIP 5

CONTROL KNOCKERS

As soon as your home is for sale, strangers knock on your door. They will ask for an immediate inspection. Under no circumstances agree.

You placed your trust in the agent. Make sure prospective buyers deal with your agent.

If you're not using an agent, ask for their details and say you'll contact them later. Now is not convenient for you.

No matter what, no matter how persuasive they are, no matter how tempted you may be, do not allow immediate entry to strangers.

Thousands of sellers lose control by letting strangers into their home. A wrong answer to an innocuous question, a negative comment, a careless quote or worse, revealing your lowest price, can all hurt you.

Some buyers will suggest "cutting out the agent". Be careful. If they cheat the agent, they'll cheat you.

Here's what to tell pesky "door-knockers"...

"Thank you but we've hired an agent to handle inspections. And besides, our home is not ready for viewing right now."

Be careful revealing your reason for selling. If it's personal and pressing, it may be used against you. Don't expect sympathy in the cruel real estate world.

The best reply when asked your reason for selling is: *"We are relocating."* That's all.

If you wish, you can add "for personal reasons". It sounds good but reveals nothing.

Aside from the value of your home, you must protect your safety.

TOP TIP 6

THE "CROWD TRAP"

Agents expose listings to hundreds of lookers who'll never buy. It's a control strategy. Pure and simple. The more people who inspect a home without buying it, the more the agent has "proof" that your price is too high.

Smart sellers don't fall for the "crowd trap".

Agents ask sellers to be absent at inspections. They say it's more comfortable for buyers. But that's not the reason. Many agents inflate inspection numbers. It's another trick from real estate school. In his book, one trainer taught: *"Stand at the door of the property with the clipboard in your hand and fill in false names."* [64]

Ironically, if large crowds show up, agents may deflate numbers. As one explained: *"If sellers think more people are interested, they want more money."* [65] But increasing a price makes a home harder to sell. Hard work is anathema to most agents. They like easy sales with less work.

Another common agents' trick is dummy offers. Nothing like fake low offers to control sellers and condition them to expect a lower price.

The official policy at one agency – and, for sure, others – is:

> After the first open inspection, each salesperson is told to "hit the vendors with a 'low-ball' fake offer".

Agents then tell the sellers: *"You need to listen to the market."* Really, the *fake* market?![66]

TYPICAL STORY: When Swinder was selling in Mosman, the agent asked her to vacate for the open home. It was during severe Covid restrictions, so Swinder parked up the street in sight of her home. She saw the agent arrive, but not a soul inspected her home. The agent later reported that "five groups came through".[67]

Swinder fired this lying agent and hired an honest agent. Fortunately, she had inserted an escape clause in the agent's agreement.

Swinder had control. Not the dodgy agent.

Smart sellers keep control with an escape clause.

TOP TIP 7
PROTECT YOUR VALUE

*"Wrong is wrong even if most are doing it.
Right is right even if few do it."*

Selling a home is nerve-racking. Nervous sellers often can't think rationally. But as agents were told by one coach:[68] *"It's your job to keep them nervous."*

Typical agents damage the value of homes; indeed, that's how they sell homes. They have never learned how to get buyers up in price, only how to bully sellers down in price.

Years ago, a Queensland TAFE teacher told students: *"Sometimes sellers need a good kick in the guts."* When I exposed this comment, he threatened me.

Another trainer (in the 2020s) brings shame to any agents with any moral compass. He tells agents to give sellers bad news – quickly and savagely.

He yells: *"F---ing tell them!"*

Swear words pour from his foul mouth. One of his printed quotes (with full swear word) is: *"F--- everyone else. It's you versus you."* He's also an auctioneer and massively undersells many homes. He constantly talks about agents' GCI (Gross Commission Income). I've never heard him mention ethics or how to protect the value of homes. He seems to delight in training agents to be cruel and unethical.

Like the voiceover at the start of the *Underbelly* television series: "It's a jungle out there."

Some so-called top salespeople are only good at being bad for sellers, such is their hubris.

Therefore, you must be determined to find an agent who understands the importance of protecting the value of your property, not trying to persuade you to sell for less.

As we often say, if you can't find a skilled, trained negotiator, consider selling your home without an agent. Again, I offer you our help.

It's a thrill when sellers reject the dodgy agents and we help them sell privately.

One memorable thrill was an 80-year-old retired headmaster who sold without an agent for more than he was quoted by agents. We then supported him to buy a smaller home. His trust and his thanks were wonderful payments. They were all we needed.

It was an honour to help you, Mr Phillips.

TOP TIP 8
BE PRICE CONFIDENT

Most agents have one strategy if a home doesn't sell in its first few weeks – drop the price.

In most cases, however, you should...

DROP THE AGENT, NOT YOUR PRICE.

The price is only one reason a home may not sell.

As long as you are not being greedy about the price for your home, if you have sound reasons to justify the price, it's important to remain confident about your home's value.

Do not be too quick to let agents shake your faith in your price.

Even if you have some doubts – and believe it, you will be under constant pressure to reduce your price – stay strong. Be proud of your home and its price.

Agents have two choices when it comes to turning a listing into a sale:

First, condition owners to reduce the price.

Second, work harder. Implement strategies that need effort.

If agents detect your price confidence waning, they will increase pressure on you. Like dogs, they can smell fear.

But if you make comments like: *"Don't worry, I'm sure you'll soon find the right buyer,"* they will try harder to get your price.

One agent jokes about reviving sellers with an oxygen mask after he's hit them to lower their prices. He enjoys pushing sellers down at auctions when they are emotional wrecks. Like many agents, he boasts about how much he gets sellers to reduce prices.

Statements such as: *"They wanted $1.8 million when we listed them. Six weeks later, we sold it for $1.25 million under the hammer,"* are common.

HOT TIP: Assertive sellers get better prices. Many Australians dislike confrontation. Comments such as, "We don't want to get the agent offside," are all too common. This is the sort of weakness that causes homes to be undersold. You don't have to be rude, but you do have to be confident and assertive. If you don't fight for your home, who will?

Don't be unrealistically stubborn, but do understand that sellers who are confident, assertive and who keep control usually get a better result.

TOP TIP 9
AVOID LAZINESS

*"Laziness travels so slowly that
poverty soon overtakes him."*

Ben Franklin

Most agents are lazy.

This is why they use auctions – to bully sellers into lowering prices and quickly selling homes.

Buyers at auction pay less than under private negotiation with a skilled negotiator.[69]

Often auction buyers resell by private negotiation after the auction.

As a young man, I bought dozens of homes at auction – mostly from the Public Trustee – and resold them for as much as twice their auction price, sometimes immediately.[70]

As explained earlier, most agents do two things: First, place an ad on the internet. Second, wait for buyers. If no buyers appear, they tell owners: *"The market says you should drop your price."*

This is the lazy way. It's also shameful.

Most agents lie, then use "the market" as an alibi to justify breaking promises.

Sellers should retort: *"Instead of me lowering my price, I'd prefer you increase your effort."*

So, be sure you know – and your agent knows (or you can direct the agent) – strategies that, while they may need more effort, will sell your property for a lot more.

Before you even think of reducing your price, make sure the agent has tried every other way to find a buyer at the right price.

A better price demands a better effort.

Lazy agents are too expensive for the simple reason that they don't do the work needed to sell homes for the best price.

That's why it's important to find that rare breed in real estate – a hard-working agent.

TOP TIP 10
HIRE A HARD-WORKING AGENT

"Most of the important things in the world have been accomplished by people who have kept on trying when there seemed to be no hope at all."

Dale Carnegie

Most of today's agents have either forgotten how to sell – or never learned. The real estate boom made it too easy for lazy agents to earn commissions.

The real worth of any agent is how that agent performs in normal times or when prices fall.

TALK TO PEOPLE – FOLLOW UP!

The first rule in selling is TTP – Talk to People. That doesn't mean waiting for people to call; it means a salesperson should call and speak with people.

You want an agent who will *chase buyers* not wait for buyers.

EXAMPLE: Scott is an agent in Melbourne. He works hard to get the best result.

As a young salesperson Scott listed an investment unit outside his usual service area.

Local agents had quoted the owner $260,000 to $280,000. But the property "owed" the owner close to $300,000. They told the owner, *"You will never get more than $300,000 because, as soon as we advertise, the buyers will see similar units for less than $300,000."*

The owner quipped: *"Well, why advertise if it will drag the price down?"*

The agents replied: *"But how can we sell it if we don't advertise?"*

Instead of using advertising, Scott used work. He decided to call investors who were clients of his agency.

He prepared a script: *"Hello, this is Scott from XYZ Real Estate; we manage a property for you. Would you be interested in another in a growth area with a great return?"*

From 20 phone calls, six investors agreed to inspect the unit. He showed it to four investors and had two offers, both above $300,000.

He sold the unit for $308,000 – almost $50,000 more than the local agent's quote.

The local agent was astounded. He asked: *"How did you get such a good price?"*

Scott replied, *"Just lucky, I guess."*

But the reason for such a great result was two words – hard work.

SIGNS OF HARD-WORKING AGENTS

- **AVAILABLE:**

    When buyers are most available, agents are available – i.e., weekends and after-hours. The agents are also easy to contact. They return calls. In my real estate days, the busiest time of year was mid-December to mid-January when other agents closed.

- **FOLLOW UP:**

    Sellers often criticise agents who pester them. And yet agents who do the most follow-up are the best agents.

    If an agent has been following you up as a seller for months, they will be just as diligent at following up buyers. That's the sort of agent you need.

Those agents you see going from door to door looking for listings, regardless of the weather – a heat wave, freezing cold, or pouring rain – are hard-working and tenacious.

Don't condemn them, admire them.

The next time there's a thunderstorm and you answer a knock on your door and a dripping agent asks when you'd like to sell, know this: That's surely the best agent in the area, one who'll work hard to get you the best price.

- **KNOWLEDGE:**

The best agents study constantly, especially on the topic of negotiation and how to better serve clients. Ask them to tell you how they can offer you a better service. If you're impressed, hire the agent. If not, reject them.

- **DIFFERENT:**

Lazy agents copy each other. You need agents who are unique, especially those committed to acting in your best interests. Be careful about being seduced by their words. Instead, look at what they do. How are they different from other agents? Importantly, how can their difference help you?

- **ACCEPT RISK:**

It takes courage and effort – plus good ethics – to accept the risks of business. Good agents know they will do a good job; they don't ask for money in advance. They know, when you see their results, that you'll be happy.

> You need agents who are unique, especially those committed to acting in your best interests.

Risk-free selling is what the best agents offer.

Find and hire these agents. Reject the others.

TOP TIP 11
CHOOSE AN AGENT
WHO TRULY PUTS YOU FIRST

"We put you first."

Meaningless misleading slogan of First National Real Estate group

Most real estate slogans are bunkum.

It doesn't matter what agents say, it doesn't matter what they promise, it doesn't matter how likeable they appear. All that matters is what they do.

Agents who keep professing their honesty are often the most dishonest. No agent admits being dodgy. No, in words, they all claim to be wonderful. It's their deeds that differ.

So, focus on what matters most: *Agents who put your interests first.* No excuses, no exceptions.

The best agents are those who willingly do:

Whatever is best for you, the sellers.

An agent in Sydney's Hills district[71] says:

"If you are not happy with me, you can sack me anytime."

An agent in Sydney's Eastern Suburbs[72] says:

"Pay me nothing until I prove what I can do for you."

An agent in Melbourne focuses entirely on clients' interests.[73]

"Our Listing Agreement has zero nasty clauses."

An agent in Brisbane offers a warranty:

"Until you are happy with our service and the price, pay nothing." [74]

All over Australia, more agents are starting to realise:

TO WIN MORE LISTINGS, BE MORE TRUSTWORTHY.

This is what you should demand of an agent:

YOU SELL OUR HOME; WE'LL PAY YOUR COMMISSION!

Only hire an agent who agrees to this condition, one who shows in *deeds* that they really do "put you first".

PART 5

15 POINTS OF CAUTION

WHAT MOST SELLERS DON'T KNOW

CAUTION POINT 1
13 UNFAIR CLAUSES IN
LISTING AGREEMENTS (CONTRACTS)

Of all the ways agents control sellers, the first and worst is their Listing Agency Agreement.

Here are 13 deadly conditions in many typical "Listing Agreements".

- **YOUR RIGHTS STRIPPED**
  You lose all rights to sell your home without paying full commission.

- **FULL COMMISSION AT LOWER PRICE**
  If your home sells for less than the price quoted, you still pay full commission.

- **ADVERTISING COSTS**
  When you agree to advertise your home, if your home does not sell, you still pay. You can lose thousands of dollars. The agent benefits from your loss.

- **KICKBACKS**
  Many agents get a bigger percentage for selling advertising (or other "extras") than for selling a house. They sanitise the word "kickback" by calling it a "rebate" – that most keep for themselves.

- **LOCKED IN REGARDLESS**
  If you are not happy with the agent, too bad, you are stuck.

- **CAVEAT**
  Some agreements give the agent (or a company such as a "Campaign Agent") the right to place a caveat on your home. Therefore, your home can't be sold until you pay the amount demanded of you.

- **UPON DEMAND** Watch for two words: "on demand". You'll be horrified what some agents can demand after you sign up.

- **DOUBLE COMMISSION**
  If you don't like this agent and choose another agent, you will have to pay two commissions – one to the agent who sells your home

and one to the agent who doesn't sell your home. Like every one of the 13 deadly clauses, it doesn't matter if this clause is unfair; what matters is that by signing up with the agent you agreed to it.

- **ENDLESS TIME**
  Dodgy agents can sign you up for four to six months.

- **CONTINUING AGENCY**
  Even when the agreement appears to expire, the agent still retains a legal hold over you. You are still controlled.

- **INTRODUCTION AGENCY**
  Many sellers don't realise that people who inspect their home with an agent "belong" to that agent. So, if hundreds of people see your home and one buys it later with another agent, you may have to pay two commissions.

- **INDEMNIFY**
  You indemnify the agent against everything that can go wrong. Even if it's the agent's fault, too bad, you are responsible.

- **NO SALE STILL PAY**
  If a sale falls through, there is a sneaky clause that forces sellers to still pay the full commission.

BUT WAIT – GOOD NEWS.

You can delete all the nasty clauses. You can also add in friendly clauses.[75]

CAUTION POINT 2
INSIST ON A GUARANTEE

"If you can't get out, don't get in."

Alec Jenman

Caveat emptor – "buyer beware" – has all but disappeared from our language thanks to the prevalence of guarantees. Consumers can now deal with most companies with confidence.

Except real estate agents.

Not only do agents not offer guarantees, but they also deliberately avoid them.

If agents were forced to give guarantees to home sellers, agents would lose the ability to lock up sellers in draconian contracts.

With guarantees, agents would lose control. Roles would be reversed. The sellers would have control.

Therefore, as a home seller, you must – no excuses, no exceptions – insist on a guarantee.

If you are not happy with the agent's service or if the agent deceives you in any way, you can then fire the agent and hire another agent.

A GUARANTEE IS YOUR GREAT ESCAPE.

Make it clear to all agents – no guarantee from them, no listing from you.

And agents, here's a tip: Offering a SERVICE GUARANTEE to sellers will revolutionise your business. Your listings will explode. Sellers will have confidence that, by offering a guarantee, you are an agent who can be trusted. You'll also be known as a smart agent.

It's good business to be good to your clients.

CAUTION POINT 3
HIDDEN SEARCH PRICES
HOW AGENTS CREATE AND CONTROL LOW OFFERS

*"I'm not upset that you lied to me,
I'm upset that from now on I can't believe you."*

Friedrich Nietzsche

Home sellers are controlled with hidden search prices. Here's how it works:

Every home for sale online has two prices. The first is the displayed price – which often says, "Contact Agent". The second is the hidden price – only known to the agents or shrewd consumers (buyers and sellers).

The hidden price means exactly that – it's the price range the agent entered when uploading details of the home.

The purpose of the hidden price is to control which buyers see a home. This is a good idea, in theory. If you have a $2 million home, don't attract buyers who can only pay $1.5 million.

But here's how sellers unknowingly lose more control:

Many agents deliberately set a low hidden price. For example, if you want $2 million, your home may show up when buyers search in the $1.5 million range. This is stark evidence of controlling conditioning.

This, of course, does exactly what sellers don't want – it attracts buyers who can only afford lower prices. And these buyers understandably make lower offers.

Once again, agents tell sellers, *"This is what the market is saying."* But, once again, the agents have attracted buyers from the wrong market.

You can't blame buyers for offering a price they've been led to believe is acceptable. Agents notoriously attract buyers from lower-priced markets. Their "buyer-nets" catch the wrong fish. As well as hidden online price ranges, thousands of buyers see homes advertised in a price range or with the words "offers above". When these buyers then offer the starting or lower price (or even the mid-point price) that's been promoted, they are met with indignation bordering on hostility.

"How dare you offer such a low price," think the sellers – as the agent grins in the background. But the buyers are only offering the price at which the home was promoted.

And the agent keeps saying, *"This is what the market is saying."*

If you've ever sold a property and wondered why you get so many offers far below the price you expect, you are likely being controlled by the agent's hidden search prices.

Here's how to discover if your agent is using the hidden price to control you.

a) Go to the website where your home is advertised.

b) Search for homes matching your home.

c) Enter a maximum price well above your home's value.

d) Slowly lower the maximum price until your home no longer appears.

The last price at which your home shows up is the *bottom* of the hidden price range.

So, if a $2 million home stops appearing at $1.5 million, the bottom of the range is $1.6 million.

The basic requirement when selling a home is to attract buyers who can afford your home.

As with other points in this book, you must inform agents that you understand hidden search prices. You know what commonly happens. This will deter most agents from attempting to control you in this manner.

CAUTION POINT 4
SELF-INTEREST AGENDAS

"In the race of life always back self-interest because, if nothing else, you always know that self-interest is trying hard."

Paul Keating

The agenda of sellers and the agenda of agents are different.

Your agenda is to sell your home at the best price.

An agent's agenda is to *sell your home*. At any price.

Research shows that the time taken to sell a home is longer when agents are selling their own homes. But when they sell your home, the time is shorter. Usually, as soon as agents get a serious offer on your home, they urge you to take it. With their own homes, they hold on longer. The same research also shows that agents get higher prices when selling their own homes.

The entire real estate industry is built around protecting the interests of agents.

If you want to control your own interests – and make sure the agent does what is best for you rather than what is best for them – focus on your self-interest.

> An agent's agenda is to sell your home. At any price.

It is not selfish to put yourself first; it's prudent.

And besides, if you do not put yourself first, who will?

Most agents can convince sellers to do things that are heavily against their best interests. They are trained at seducing and controlling sellers. It's all about them.

The common ways agents seduce sellers into acting against their best interests are:

1. SELLING BY PUBLIC AUCTION

Agents who tell sellers that "auction is the best way to get the best price" are either incompetent or dishonest (foolish or crooked). There can be no other excuse for using a method that so brazenly causes sellers to undersell their homes.

2. VPA – VENDOR PAID ADVERTISING

As already discussed, every agent now persuades almost every seller to pay for advertising. The greatest scam of all is how sellers are convinced to upgrade to a premium ad for thousands of dollars extra. Yet inexpensive ads are often more effective.

3. ADVERTISING IS CONDITIONING

While it benefits agents to be seen on many websites, the last thing sellers need is buyers saying: *"Gee, we see this home everywhere."*

The more advertising that gets done and the longer the home remains unsold, the lower the price becomes – and the easier the home is to sell. And the sooner the agents get paid.

WARNING:

DON'T LET YOUR HOME BECOME A LEMON

When homes turn into "lemons", their value can fall substantially.

There are two main ways homes turn into "lemons":

ONE: AUCTION LEMONS

Auctions are the best way for agents to control sellers – that's why agents lie and say that auctions are the best way to sell.

Auction figures are skewed to make auctions appear successful. The real clearance rate rarely exceeds 50 percent.

But let's say that 70% of homes put to auction do sell at the auctions. That means, if you are persuaded to use auction, there is a 30 percent chance your home will fail to sell *at* the auction. It then becomes an "Auction Lemon".

And if you think that you got pressured to lower your price before an auction, the pressure will be much higher if you fail to sell at auction.

Don't risk your home becoming an auction lemon. Don't auction.

IMPORTANT POINT: Buyers don't buy homes because they are auctioned; they buy because they like the homes. Almost all buyers detest auctions.

TWO: ADVERTISING LEMONS

Homes that are advertised are often the second-best homes. The best homes are snapped up by waiting buyers, often for massive prices.

The moment any home is advertised, its price is on a downward path until, having been advertised too long, it becomes an ADVERTISING LEMON.

Be careful. Advertising should usually be your last action, not your first.

4. FAKE "NOISE"

Agents often get pressured by sellers to create "noise" – lots of open inspections, lots of advertising, lots of comments, lots of promises, lots of interested buyers. And best of all, lots of good offers.

It all adds up to what most people desire in life – hope. But what good is false hope?

In real estate, too much "noise" damages a home's value.

If there are few or, worse, no inspections, sellers panic. Many sellers get angry with an agent who appears to be "doing nothing". But if there is no qualified buyer available to inspect a home today, what is the agent supposed to do?

Sellers can't see the work an agent does behind-the-scenes like following up buyers – as good agents do. So consequently, some sellers get angry with a good agent because they have "heard nothing". But hearing nothing does not mean nothing is happening.

But here's what agents do – and for two reasons: first, to placate the owners and second, to further condition the owners – they create FAKE NOISE.

Don't pressure an agent to create noise. It's hard enough to get the best price when you know the truth. With lies, fake figures and tyre-kickers, it's harder to get a good result.

Sometimes your best strategy is to wait it out. The right buyer *will* arrive. One day.

BEWARE THE TIME TRAP

If you can't wait – and the agent has worked hard and tried everything possible – then you may have only two choices. Withdraw your home from sale. Or accept the best offer available – knowing, of course, that it will be the highest price at this time.

But this is where stubborn sellers make a grave mistake. They think they have a third choice – a different agent. This usually leads to disaster and a lower price.

Agents never deliberately *don't* sell homes. If a good agent doesn't get the price you want, then that price is probably not possible right now. A second agent is unlikely to do better.

Indeed, the reason second and third agents often sell homes for less than the first agent is because, in real estate, time is often your enemy. The longer you wait, the less you get.

5. THE PRESSURE OF "OFFERS"

There are few things worse when selling your home than pressure to "take an offer".

When it comes to offers, agents are great persuaders – not at getting buyers up in price but in getting sellers down in price. Before considering any offer, always ask yourself: *Is this really the BHP (Buyers' Highest Price)?* (See Caution Point 5 – RULES FOR OFFERS)

12 PRESSURE STATEMENTS AGENTS USE ON SELLERS

1. *"I know it's less than you expected, but it's what the market is telling us."*
2. *"These buyers are at their limit."*
3. *"The buyers have to spend money to renovate your home."*
4. *"They originally offered a lot less. I got them up to this price."*
5. *"If you refuse this offer, the next offer could be less."*
6. *"With high interest rates buyers can't borrow as much."*
7. *"We've had 36 inspections; this is the first (or best) serious offer."*
8. *"Your home has been 'viewed' thousands of times online."*
9. *"If you don't sell soon, people will think something's wrong or it's too dear."*
10. *"It could be months – even years – before you get another offer as good."*
11. *"They're looking at another property – it's for auction and they expect to buy it cheap."*
12. *"They need an answer by 5 o'clock today – otherwise they'll withdraw their offer."*

BE CAREFUL: Many sellers hear one or more of these statements. They feel the pressure, the doubt, the awful thought of what could happen if they say no.

In most cases, if you are being pushed to accept an offer: DO NOT BE RUSHED.

TAKE YOUR TIME,
THINK CAREFULLY ABOUT OFFERS

CAUTION POINT 5
RULES FOR OFFERS

*"You don't get what you deserve,
you get what you negotiate."*

Chester L Karrass,
author of The Negotiating Game

12 BEST RULES OF REAL ESTATE OFFERS

RULE 1: OBEY THE LAW – strictly.

Most agents routinely break laws.

From minor puffery to major fraud, real estate is riddled with scoundrels.

Many times, both buyers and sellers are coerced into breaking the law by agents who say, *"Trust me, I have been doing this for years."*

For example, dodgy agents persuade sellers to sanction bait-pricing (offering homes at a misleading low price to attract more buyers).

And not all lawbreakers are agents.

No matter how innocuous, never trust anyone who suggests any illegal scheme. People who cheat in one aspect of their lives cheat in all aspects. Cheaters are cheaters. Agents who cheat buyers also cheat sellers – indeed, bait-pricing which, at first, seems to be cheating buyers is also cheating sellers (as it forces their price down).

Why would you trust an agent who admits to cheating for "years"? It makes no sense.

Aside from cheating one (or more) of the three main participants in a property sale – sellers, buyers and agents – all three often think it's okay to cheat the government. Or the lenders.

From stamp duty avoidance to falsely claiming the first home-buyers grant, some people leap into lawbreaking with nary a thought about risks or penalties. Breaking the law is a criminal offence. People who commit criminal offences go to jail. Plus, there is another huge risk with breaking the law – the pain you could bring on yourself.[76]

There are two "types" of laws – legal and moral. From sellers who exaggerate to buyers who invent sob stories to sleazy agents who have illicit sex in clients' homes,[77] all are breaking moral laws.

If you want to be treated fairly, vow to treat others fairly. You may not always be treated similarly, but at least you won't go to jail or lose your home. Or feel bad.

RULE 2: THE MOST IMPORTANT QUESTION!

Before you decide whether to accept an offer, the first – and most important – question is:

"Will accepting this offer make our lives better?"

If not, REJECT the offer.

If yes, ACCEPT the offer, **PROVIDED THAT** it's the …

BHP

(Buyers' Highest Price).

Confirmed with a Buyers' Price Declaration (See Rule 12).

RULE 3: BE A KNOW-ALL (or know one!)

There's a saying: *"If you think education is expensive, try ignorance."* Nowhere is your knowledge of negotiation – even basic negotiation knowledge – more important than when negotiating with a serious buyer. The more you know, the higher the offers will go.

You must read the 28-page booklet ***the 42 Rules of Real Estate Negotiation.*** Within minutes, you'll see how you (or your agent) can persuade buyers to increase offers. Be sure your agent knows and understands these rules. You can download them at jenman.com.au.

To keep control, ask the agent: *"Which of the 42 rules have you used with these buyers?"* This is especially important when agents say (as many do): *"The buyers won't go higher."*

Another great question to ask agents who claim buyers won't increase an offer is this:

> When it comes to their own money, agents are more careful.

"If I [or my supporter] speak with the buyers and convince them to do what you say they won't do – increase their offer – will you agree to forfeit your commission?"

If the agent says no – as most will – you reply: *"But you just told me the buyers definitely won't pay more."* When it comes to their own money, agents are more careful. It's called self-interest.

When agents push you to accept a lower offer, push them to get a higher offer. Stand up for yourself. It's in your self-interest.[78]

RULE 4: NEVER ACCEPT THREATS

Never deal with anyone who threatens you. There is nothing worse than the pressure of a deadline or a threat. A deadline – especially without courtesy – is one notch above a threat. Tell the agent that you will not negotiate with any form of threat. Your response can be simple: *"Withdraw all threats and then start negotiating, nicely. Thank you."*

RULE 5: THE BUYER IS THE SOLUTION

After decades of research and experience, I can assure you that in most cases the secret to success in real estate negotiations is usually with the buyers. Yet, agents place more focus on pushing sellers down than lifting buyers up. Tell agents, *"Focus on the buyers, not me."*

RULE 6: BE THE MOST POWERFUL

Those with the most power get the best deal. And the most powerful person in a negotiation is the one most prepared to walk away. Don't be rude about it, but if you act like it doesn't matter too much if they don't buy (at or above your price), the buyers will be more likely to pay your price. Especially if they love your home and you give them your "Love List".[79]

RULE 7: FORGET PRESSURE, REMEMBER BUSES

People who pressure you to make a fast decision are doing it for their benefit not yours. Consider this: In many cases, if one buyer makes an offer at a certain price, it's likely there'll soon be another buyer at the same price – or an even better price. Especially in a rising or booming market. Think of buyers like buses: if you miss one, another will soon be along.

RULE 8: YOU STILL OWN THE HOME

If you lose the buyer, don't feel like a loser. You didn't lose your home. If the buyers reject your home – for whatever reason – you keep your home. And, if it's a beautiful home in a sought-after area, your agent should soon find another buyer.[80]

RULE 9: SHOW ME THE MONEY!

Be careful. Some buyers make off-the-cuff offers. They are not serious; they just want to discover your lowest price. Only negotiate with serious buyers. And serious buyers gladly pay a deposit – and sign a contract. Indeed, the more money they pay as a deposit, the more serious they are likely to be.

NEVER START NEGOTIATING UNLESS THE BUYERS HAVE PAID MONEY AS A SIGN OF THEIR SERIOUSNESS.

And don't fall for the line: *"If you accept our offer, we'll pay a deposit."* Pay now. You have shown your home; it's time to show their money. No money, no negotiation.

RULE 10. INSTEAD OF DROPPING, CONSIDER "CARRYING"

Let's say you are asking $2.5 million for your home. Confidentially, you'd accept $2.2 million. And let's say that some buyers tell you their borrowing capacity only allows them to pay $2.2 million.

Your first instinct will be to accept – after all, it's the price you expected.

BUT...

Rather than instantly accept, reply: *"So if you could borrow $2.5 million, you'd pay that price?"*

They should say yes; after all, they said they're limited by what they can borrow.

So, instead of dropping $300,000, offer to "carry $300,000".

This means you lend the buyers $300,000 which they repay over, say, ten years at $30,000 a year. Instead of giving away $300,000 (even if you are willing to do so) you will now receive about $600 per week for ten years.[81]

This is known as "vendor finance" and is more common than most sellers realise,[82] especially on rural properties where loans are often harder to obtain.

Be sure you get competent independent legal advice and comply with all laws.[83]

RULE 11. CONSIDER TERMS

There are two components to selling a home for a great result. Most people, especially agents, only consider one component – the price.

The second component is "terms".

"Terms" means offering some special benefits or conditions that appeal to buyers. For example, allowing buyers early access to the property which may save them having to make three moves and pay large rent. Or offering a delayed settlement while buyers sell another asset to raise the cash to pay a good price for the home.

Even offering to leave some "extras" which may normally be excluded can "sweeten" the deal for buyers. Extras may include items such as pool cleaning equipment, dishwashers, even furniture. Small offerings can clinch a big sale.

Now, granted, the agent gets no real benefit from the terms of the sale. This is why agents only focus on money – it leads straight to their commission. Indeed, in some cases, agents will even advocate methods of sale that eliminate or reduce terms or, worse, make terms so onerous as to repel the best buyers. For example, auctions. Agents say that you get a contract with no conditions at auctions. But many buyers need conditions.

It generally costs little or nothing to accommodate the wishes of the other parties. Being kind and considerate gets a better result than being hard and ruthless, that's for sure.[84]

Always remember to be kind and considerate towards the needs and wishes of the buyers. Some agents make a habit of creating confrontation between buyers and sellers. If the agent is referring to buyers as "the buyers", that's not as personal as referring to them by their names.

Being introduced to the buyers can also facilitate a smooth and successful negotiation. Most people don't want to move into a home where there was animosity towards them from the previous occupants.

A home is supposed to be a place of warmth and happiness. Treat negotiations in the same manner and you'll achieve a better result – in price and terms.

And, of course, in happiness.

RULE 12. DISCOVER THE BHP (BUYERS' HIGHEST PRICE)

Nothing is more important when selling your property than ensuring you get the highest market price. Anything less means you've undersold.

Look at it this way: If you had two million dollars in the bank, how much would you want if you closed your account?

Would you be happy with $1.8 million? What about $1.9 million?

Of course not.

Whatever money you have in your bank account, that's the amount you will insist on being paid if you decide to close your bank account. Not a cent less.

Surely the same should apply with your home.

If your home is worth two million dollars, why would you consider selling it below its value? You wouldn't succumb to pressure from a bank manager. So don't succumb to pressure from a real estate agent.

The reason most (about 90%[85]) of properties are undersold is because...

MOST AGENTS FOCUS ON THE WRONG PRICE.

There are two prices in every sale:

The first is the **SELLERS' LOWEST PRICE** (in auctions, called "Reserve Price").

From the moment agents meet sellers, they want an answer to one question: *What is the lowest price the sellers will accept?*

Of course, once agents know the sellers' lowest price, that becomes their major focus. If they think – as they usually do – that the sellers' lowest price is too high, the agents will condition the sellers down in price.

Most sales occur when sellers agree to accept a certain price – usually their minimum. It's common for sellers to say to agents: *"I won't go any lower than X dollars."* And that – or lower – then becomes the final sale price.

Here is the **BIG PRICE QUESTION** to ask agents:

HOW DO YOU KNOW THAT THE BUYERS' OFFER IS THE MOST THEY ARE WILLING TO PAY?

The second price (after the sellers' lowest price) is …

THE BUYERS' HIGHEST PRICE

aka

The BHP

Most agents never discover the buyers' highest price. This is why most agents undersell the homes (even though they have a fiduciary duty to act in the sellers' best interests).

How can you sell a home for the best price unless you know the Buyers' Highest Price?

So, how do you discover the BHP? Simple – you find an agent skilled at negotiation.

And how do these agents obtain the highest price from buyers?

They use a document first designed (many years ago when he was a successful agent[86]) by Australia's best real estate trainer, Michael Kies:

A BUYERS' PRICE DECLARATION[87]

Buyers' Price Declaration

1. We have inspected the property located at:

....
Address of Property

2. Following discussions with the seller's agent, we advise that we are **interested in buying the property** subject to any further independent advice which we may seek.

3. The HIGHEST price we are prepared to pay for the property is...

.... $..............
Price to be written in words as well as in numbers.

4. We also advise that should someone else offer a price for this property that is HIGHER than the price stated above (in Point 3), we will NOT increase our price. The price stated is the **Highest Price** we are prepared to pay.

5. In order to demonstrate both the sincerity and the FINALITY of our price, we declare that we do NOT require notification should another buyer offer a price higher than that offered by us. In such event, we understand that the property may be **immediately sold to the other buyer.** We will NOT pay more than the price already stated, therefore we do not require an opportunity to increase our price.

6. This declaration does not place any legal obligation upon us to purchase the property, even at the price stated above. Until such time as a formal contract has been signed by both the seller and us, there is no legal obligation for us to buy or for the seller to sell. We also understand that the amount of our maximum price will not be revealed to any person other than the agent and the seller.

Name: ....

Signature: .... Date: ....

By signing this declaration, I acknowledge that:

a) I have been given a copy of it; and
b) that I have been advised to seek independent advice.

Please note: Although this Declaration is designed by The Jenman Group, the agent using it is not necessarily a Jenman APPROVED agent. For any enquiries please call 1800 1800 18 or visit www.jenman.com. Thank you.

© Neil Jenman 2001

CAUTION POINT 6
THE PAUSE BUTTON

When you look back at your biggest mistakes in life, there is usually something you discover: Lack of thought. Well, if there is one time in life when you need to "pause" and THINK IT OVER, surely that time is when you are considering the sale of your biggest financial asset.

Whenever you are feeling stressed or a bit rushed, especially if you are being pressured and you just don't feel right, consider a technique that can save you plenty of later pain...

PUSH THE PAUSE BUTTON

Just say – to anyone who's hassling you: *"We are going to push the pause button. We need more time to think it over."* Those three words – THINK IT OVER – combined with the strategy of "pushing the pause button" can have a major positive impact on your financial life.

But be careful: Many agents are trained in "how to overcome the think-it-over excuse".[88]

So, stay firm in your decision. You need more time to think things over. You are pushing the pause button. Any agent who does not respect your decision is an agent you must reject.

CAUTION POINT 7
A SECRET VALUATION

Only a registered valuer can give you a "valuation". Agents can only give you a "market appraisal". And, unless agents inflate the sale price of a property, most sellers will reject them. Agents know the great truth of winning listings: *The biggest liars win the listing.*

Many home sellers, therefore, find it comforting to pay for a valuation on their homes. Unlike agents, valuers do not have a vested interest in the price quoted for your home. You pay for their professional opinion. No matter what you feel about the amount of their valuation, you still pay their fees. This means that valuers are more honest and accurate than agents. Not always, but most times.

You are not obligated to disclose the valuation to anyone. It's for your private purposes. It helps you to get a more realistic idea of the true value of your home. Please remember the saying, "Truth hurts", so don't get angry with the valuer.

To be sure, valuers are not always right, although, as stated, they are usually more accurate than agents. Valuers have done a five year university course. Not so agents. The cost of a few hundred dollars in a valuation can be a good investment.

CAUTION POINT 8
AVOID MOST AGENT-FINDERS

If you haven't seen Dick Smith's video[89] exposing accommodation booking companies, you must find it. You'll be appalled at how these companies (most foreign) make so much money for doing so little – and send small Aussie business owners (like country motels) to the wall.

Something similar has sprung up in real estate.

The internet is filled with companies promising to help home sellers find the best agents.

Or compare local agents.

Or compare commission rates.

Like so much in real estate, it's misleading and deceptive. And mostly nonsense.

These companies have one goal – to get a spotter's fee from agents. They care nothing about protecting you. They impose no conditions on agents to care for you. They have no quality control process. Any advice they give you is skewed in favour of agents. Greed incites treachery – and most of these companies are mighty greedy. They will shaft you as quick as it takes you to hit the "learn more" symbol.

> You are better off going direct to an agent.

All they do is get your name and details and "shop you" out to many agents, all of whom are bound to pay them a spotter's fee when you sell.

And then, whichever agent sells your home – at whatever price or conditions – regardless of whether you are happy or miserable, the agents get their commission, and the agent-finder company gets their lead-generation fee.

Be careful. Just like the accommodation booking companies that Dick Smith rails against, this is a neat stitch-up motivated by pure greed. These companies do nothing you couldn't do for yourself – and often get a much better deal.

The best agents often refuse to work with agent-finding companies.

Rather than using these companies you are better off going direct to an agent OR finding a true vendor advocate who will focus on your best interests.[90]

Just as both you and the motel owners will be better off if you avoid those motel-finding and booking companies.

CAUTION POINT 9

SHOULD YOU "STAGE" OR RENOVATE/REPAIR?

Over the past few years, "staging" has become common. But is staging worth it?

Well, provided the home's value increases more than the cost of the staging, yes, it is worth it.

Here's what I feel: Buyers are wary of anything fake. So, if your home presents beautifully, if it already has a feeling of love and warmth, why change it?

If, however, your home needs a freshen up, staging can be a good investment.

Scott Kim is an up-and-coming agent in Melbourne. As of 2024, he is someone in whom I have total trust.[91] One of the best I have ever known.

I asked Scott for his opinion on the phenomenon of staging – or styling as some call it. (Styling sounds less fake than staging.)

Here is an extract from Scott's reply:[92]

It can very well be worth staging a home.

Staging gives a home a sense of "modernness". Most homes are a mix of old and new. A good stylist brings appropriately sized furniture, with appropriate colour schemes. This can really make a home flow better. In most instances, it creates additional space that homes need (as most homes have oversized furniture designed for comfort, but styled homes have ideal sized furniture, so bedrooms and living areas are maximised). Styling can greatly increase a home's value. I believe that for every $1 spent, you get three to five dollars.

Scott gave many examples where styling (and renovations) increased values of homes; usually, with styling alone, by at least $50,000. In one case, sellers received almost $400,000 extra following Scott's advice on renovations and styling.[93]

Here's the rule: For every dollar spent, you need three dollars back, hopefully more.

A final tip: Does the agent get commission from the staging company? If so, forget it – or use their commission as a discount to you. Unless they arrange and supervise a major renovation, the commission on the sale of a property should be sufficient for agents.[94]

CAUTION POINT 10
IF YOU MUST ADVERTISE

Brent Courtney was one of the best agents – with "best" meaning caring for clients. Although with a franchise, his personal values did not match many dictums of the franchise.

Brent's franchise had a policy where all home sellers – regardless of circumstances – were forced to pay at least $5,000 for premium advertising. Many times, Brent skipped advertising. He achieved superb prices through his contacts which led to excellent off-market sales.

In 2020 a lovely doctor contacted me. He said, *"I have a pathological hatred of agents."* The doctor was selling a family home in Lane Cove. I suggested Brent Courtney.

As often happens when agents have buyers on their books, there was a flurry of early interest and several offers. Finally, the price of $2 million was reached. While that figure may have satisfied the doctor, Brent was an agent who didn't stop once owners agreed to sell. He believed in finding the best buyers and getting them to pay their best price.

Soon, he managed to negotiate the price up to a mammoth $2.2 million. The doctor was delighted. Brent was rightly proud. It was a great result for an old home on a tiny block.

But I was worried that despite getting more than expected, we may have been able to achieve even more. This was during the huge Sydney boom of the early 2020s.

I asked Brent to place a small ad on the internet. In a tone that revealed a mix of shame and embarrassment, Brent said he was "not allowed" to place a small ad.

Brent explained that, under the rules of his franchise,[95] the minimum advertising spend for this office had to be $5000. I got upset. I said that if he could not do as I requested, I would find another agent. Or worse (for him), fire him and help the owner sell without an agent.[96]

Brent defied his franchise. He placed an inexpensive ad online. It worked. He found another buyer who offered $2.4 million. The owner was rapt. He received $200,000 more than he had already accepted.

Brent was now an agent the doctor admired – for his integrity and his negotiation skill. Plus, of course, his focus on client care. A good man.

Thank you, Brent Courtney, for standing up to the esurient policy of your franchise. If only there were more agents like you.[97]

CAUTION POINT 11
"JENMAN AGENTS"

When I say 93% of agents can't be trusted, I often include agents who purport to be "Jenman agents".

Of all the frustrations in my real estate career, the worst is agents who pretend to support my campaign to protect consumers.

I resent being the "Trojan Horse" for agents to meet – and sign up – sellers, and then contravene every principle I espouse. It's not only embarrassing to me and my family – and those agents who genuinely support our ethics in real estate – it's near fraudulent and certainly hypocritical to claim to support Jenman, or to be a "Jenman Approved" agent, and not abide by our Codes of Ethics and our Codes of Client Care (both available online at jenman.com.au).

If you are selling and an agent claims to be a "Jenman agent", don't instantly sign up. Instead...

CHECK WITH US FIRST.

Call 1800 1800 18 or email support@jenman.com.au

If you hire a "Jenman Approved" agent or any agent who claims to support our codes, and you are treated badly, please let us know.

In many cases, we can help you escape from the control of dodgy agents.[98]

CAUTION POINT 12
SELL OR BUY –
WHICH COMES FIRST?

It's one of the most common challenges for real estate consumers:

Do you sell first and buy later?

OR

Do you buy first and sell later?

Both options come with risks and frightening dangers.

If you sell first – and can't find somewhere to buy – you'll have nowhere to live. Although "homelessness" might be extreme, even the thought of not having a home is terrifying.

If you buy first – then can't sell your home – you may have to slash your price and take a loss. Or you may have to pay expensive bridging finance. Or worse, forfeit the deposit on your purchase and be sued for specific performance; that's an unthinkable alternative.

The best and safest solution is to …

SELL AND BUY SIMULTANEOUSLY

Remember "Rule 11 of the 12 Rules for offers – **TERMS**.

As well as the price, you can set the terms under which you sell. You simply make the sale of your home subject to you finding another home.

This is quite common. It's known as a …

"SUBJECT TO" sale.

While agents may not like this – as it slows their commission – it's eminently practical. And it certainly provides you with peace of mind.

And don't take much notice if agents say this idea will "repel buyers". If buyers love your home (and plan to live in it for many years), they will be quite willing to wait a few weeks – even a couple of months – before they move in.

Provided, of course, you are fair and reasonable. (Remember Top Tip 1 – "Be kind to buyers".)

As with so much else, be sure you...
GET INDEPENDENT LEGAL ADVICE
FROM A COMPETENT LAWYER.

CAUTION POINT 13
TRANSPARENCY TRAP

One of the most seductive words in real estate is "transparency".

Agents will boast that their methods are "totally transparent" and therefore fair to everyone.

But while transparency may be good for buyers and agents, it can be financially bad for sellers.

The classic example is public auctions or online auctions (such as "Openn Negotiation"). In these flawed methods of sale, buyers make their offers in public.

This so-called "transparency" creates the ludicrous situation where all buyers can see how much every other buyer is offering.

And sure, this is transparent. But it is also stupid – from a negotiation perspective.

When buyers can see what other buyers are offering, instead of offering their highest price (the BHP), they only offer a small amount above the buyer beneath them. This means that properties are undersold due to transparency.

Imagine a government tender process where construction companies are bidding to build, say, a motorway. If the person in charge of monitoring bids was to disclose to each bidder the amount offered by all bidders, this would be a criminal offence.

CAUTION POINT 12
SELL OR BUY –
WHICH COMES FIRST?

It's one of the most common challenges for real estate consumers:

Do you sell first and buy later?

OR

Do you buy first and sell later?

Both options come with risks and frightening dangers.

If you sell first – and can't find somewhere to buy – you'll have nowhere to live. Although "homelessness" might be extreme, even the thought of not having a home is terrifying.

If you buy first – then can't sell your home – you may have to slash your price and take a loss. Or you may have to pay expensive bridging finance. Or worse, forfeit the deposit on your purchase and be sued for specific performance; that's an unthinkable alternative.

The best and safest solution is to …

SELL AND BUY SIMULTANEOUSLY

Remember "Rule 11 of the 12 Rules for offers – **TERMS**.

As well as the price, you can set the terms under which you sell. You simply make the sale of your home subject to you finding another home.

This is quite common. It's known as a …

"SUBJECT TO" sale.

While agents may not like this – as it slows their commission – it's eminently practical. And it certainly provides you with peace of mind.

And don't take much notice if agents say this idea will "repel buyers". If buyers love your home (and plan to live in it for many years), they will be quite willing to wait a few weeks – even a couple of months – before they move in.

Provided, of course, you are fair and reasonable. (Remember Top Tip 1 – "Be kind to buyers".)

As with so much else, be sure you...
GET INDEPENDENT LEGAL ADVICE
FROM A COMPETENT LAWYER.

CAUTION POINT 13
TRANSPARENCY TRAP

One of the most seductive words in real estate is "transparency".

Agents will boast that their methods are "totally transparent" and therefore fair to everyone.

But while transparency may be good for buyers and agents, it can be financially bad for sellers.

The classic example is public auctions or online auctions (such as "Openn Negotiation"). In these flawed methods of sale, buyers make their offers in public.

This so-called "transparency" creates the ludicrous situation where all buyers can see how much every other buyer is offering.

And sure, this is transparent. But it is also stupid – from a negotiation perspective.

When buyers can see what other buyers are offering, instead of offering their highest price (the BHP), they only offer a small amount above the buyer beneath them. This means that properties are undersold due to transparency.

Imagine a government tender process where construction companies are bidding to build, say, a motorway. If the person in charge of monitoring bids was to disclose to each bidder the amount offered by all bidders, this would be a criminal offence.

And yet this sort of "transparency" is what many agents do all the time.

Reject "transparency". In negotiation, the way to achieve the highest price is **PRIVACY**.

Imagine going to a casino, playing cards, and insisting that players comply with your desire for "transparency". You'd be ridiculed. Or banned from the casino.

ILLUSTRATIVE STORY: Many years ago, I met with the then NSW Minister for Fair Trading, John Watkins.[99] I explained the widespread fraud in real estate auctions. I must have become passionate because suddenly Mr Watkins said: *"Mr Jenman, I am not going to ban auctions."*

I replied, *"No, of course not. Just make real estate auctions safe for consumers."*

He said, *"Exactly."*

I retorted, *"Well, then you'll have to ban auctions."*

We both smiled sadly.

CAUTION POINT 14
THE PRICE DELUSION PRICE TRAP

All homeowners want the best price when they sell. Nothing wrong with this, you might think. Aren't we entitled to the best price? Well yes, of course. It's not greedy to want the best price, it's prudent.

The trouble is, however, that if you ask too high a price for your home, you could lose thousands of dollars. Take care. Think it over.

It's a real estate truth: If you start too high (an impossible-to-achieve price), you'll surely sell too low.

Here's what happens: A property is offered for sale above its value. Buyers who should see it never see it. Eventually, it undersells.

For example, let's say the true value of a property is around $1,900,000. Many owners over-price their properties by at least 20 percent, often more. A $1,900,000 property goes on the market for well over $2 million, maybe $2.25 million. In extreme cases (not uncommon) a property worth around $1.9 million is first offered for sale at $2.5 million.

Home sellers often say: *"If we start high, we can always come down later."* But if they start too high, they'll be forced to come crashing down later.

Don't think that hiding the price – or choosing auction – means you'll disguise the price. The more you try to avoid the price issue, the more suspicion you create. Buyers instantly think "over-priced". And don't allow an agent to use a bait price; all that does is encourage buyers to pay less for your home.

These days, buyers shop around like never before; they spend hours online. They can soon spot an over-priced property in a couple of mouse clicks.

Buyers laugh at over-priced properties. Hardly any inspect such properties. So, a few weeks later, when sellers realise that buyers don't share their inflated opinion of their home, it's too late. The damage is done. The property is now a lemon.

So, instead of reducing the price to its true value of, say, $1,900,000, the sellers may find themselves forced to reduce the price even lower to attract a buyer. Consequently, a home that should have sold for $1,900,000 may sell for $1,800,000 (or lower) – all because it was too high at the start.

> **Over-priced properties usually become under-priced sales.**

A study (from the United States in 2009) revealed that when most homeowners think of the value of their own homes, they are "bordering on delusional".[100]

So, be careful. Over-priced homes can languish for months. The sellers don't realise the damage to their home's value. First, buyers ignore over-priced homes; then they laugh. Over-priced properties usually become under-priced sales.

Don't fall for the Price Delusion Trap.

Price your property right. And then sell it for the best price.

IMPORTANT AND OBVIOUS POINT: Don't worry. One sure way to know if you've priced your property too low is if you get more than one buyer interested.

In such circumstances, the Buyers' Price Declaration (see Caution Point 5 – Rule 12) will get you the highest and best price.

A sure way to know if you've priced your property too high is when you get no interest. If the agent has worked hard, then the reason for no interest is the price. Even the worst skilled and most dishonest agents want to sell your home. If there is no interest, check your price expectations.

And sure, some sellers are quick to say, *"But the house up the street sold for more than we are asking, and our place is much better."*

Well, if your property hasn't sold, it means buyers don't agree with you. As agents, valuers and most industry figures often say: "A property is only worth what a buyer will pay."

Not quite. I prefer to say: *"A property is worth what a good agent can persuade a buyer to pay."*

CAUTION POINT 15
AVOID CREATING ENEMIES!

When searching for an agent to sell your home, don't allow too many agents to inspect your home. Check them out by phone first. Or mystery shop them.

Some sellers get some sort of perverse delight from having every agent in their area inspecting their home and seeing the agents grovelling (near-begging) to be the chosen agent. These sellers enjoy the feeling of power they possess. But, believe it, it's only short term.

Those fawning and obsequious agents can be your worst enemy when you reject them.

Here's the problem: If you call ten agents, you'll soon have ten "pests". All telling you they're the best, all offering lower commission or no marketing expenses. Your head will spin.

Often, the worst agents promise the most. Some make you feel guilty if you think of not choosing them.

But guess what?

When you finally choose one agent, you don't realise that you've just created nine enemies; many will savagely resent you for not choosing them.

And because they've all seen your home, they'll mention its faults to buyers.

Given that most buyers "circulate" in an area, you should not let more than one or two (three at most) agents inspect your home.

You don't need to let every agent inspect your home. Check them out from a distance, then short list them down to two or three to inspect your home.

Ideally, only one – the best one. And don't make the mistake of choosing agents with the biggest profile (ego).

It can't be stressed often enough. A top agent often means a bottom price. Just because agents sell a lot, it does not mean they are getting a lot for the homes they sell. Often, it's the opposite.

Agents who make lots of sales are either very good or very bad, at least when it comes to caring for their clients. Being good at control, conditioning or bullying you down in price is not what you want in an agent.

Study agents carefully – from a distance. Ask around – especially among your close friends or those in the industry in whom you have high trust and know they'll protect your interests.

PART 6

EXTRA CONTROL

One of the hardest challenges when writing a book is knowing what to include or exclude. If a book is too large, it tends to intimidate. People say, "I don't have time to read that!"

But consider this:

It takes a minute to read one page. Let's say two minutes if you highlight points of interest. This book is around 130 pages – so it will take you, at most, 240 minutes to read it.

That's four hours.

Surely, you can find four hours – that's 30 minutes a day for eight days – to acquire the knowledge to control agents instead of agents controlling you.

Most homes are undersold because agents know more about controlling sellers than sellers know about controlling agents.

So, well done – if you have read this far into this book. You deserve a great result.

If you have any further questions, comments or concerns after reading this book, please feel welcome to contact me, the author, or my son and co-author Alec Jenman on alec@jenman.com.au. Or any of our colleagues on support@jenman.com.au

I never want to stop helping decent home sellers, especially those who are appreciative.

So, to that end, here are some more tips to help you...

✓ PATIENCE IS PARAMOUNT

Patience truly is a virtue. It can also be profitable.

Many times, sellers panic – or crack under pressure – and sell their homes too cheaply.

If your agent is working hard, maybe the right buyer is just not around right now. As Australia's best real estate coach, Michael Kies, often advises sellers and agents (especially those getting too pushy with sellers):

"It's just going to take a little longer, that's all."

When faced between a choice of drop your price or wait, it often pays to wait.

Here's a great point about patience: Let's say you want to sell your home for $2.5 million. The agent is bringing you offers near $2 million. Consider this: If a buyer said: *"I'm happy to buy your home for $2.45 million and I will sign a contract today which guarantees that you will be paid BUT it will be nine months before I can complete the purchase."*

Would you accept such an offer? Many sellers would say *"Yes"*.

To which I would reply, *"Well, that's the same as waiting nine months."*

I once used this point with sellers of a lovely home on Sydney's North Shore. As a direct result of their patience – and rejecting many offers of $5.5 million (and slightly above) – a few months later they had two eager buyers. One offered $7.2 million. The other offered $7.5 million.

Never had the words "WORTH THE WAIT" seemed so true.

✓ YOU ARE NOT A "BUYER"

If the agent is bringing you low offers from buyers, consider this logical reply:

"These are not buyers; they are just offerors."

If anyone – especially agents – tries to make you feel like a failure because, according to them, you have "failed to sell", correct them. Just reply:

"We have not failed to sell. We have refused to sell at a low price some buyers offered. We could sell tomorrow. But we want to sell for the right price, thank you".

✓ "AM I TOO GREEDY?"

Agents often describe sellers as "greedy". Most times, however, the sellers are only expecting the price the agent quoted them before they listed. The chutzpah of most agents is astounding.

There is nothing greedy about wanting the right price. And there is nothing greedy about expecting agents to keep promises. *"You said it, you get it,"* is a statement more sellers need to throw at agents. Never be frightened of "offending" dodgy agents.

Such as when agents tell sellers to "lower your expectations", the sellers can tell the agent: *"Oh, our expectations are lowered alright; but of you, not our price."*

Geoff Lane owned a gorgeous home in Roseville. Before he listed, some agents quoted him above $5 million. Geoff figured his home was not worth more than $5 million. As weeks turned into months and agents were bringing him offers of around $4.2 million and urging him to "be realistic" and "listen to the market", Geoff asked himself the following questions:

- *Is it unrealistic to expect the price the agent quoted me before I listed?*
- *Is "the market" comprised of these low offers the agents are now bringing me?*

And then Geoff asked himself a question befitting a man of character:
- *Am I too greedy?*

I visited Geoff and his partner Barbara at their home. He asked me if he was being too greedy. I did not believe so. I felt his agent lacked the knowledge to negotiate the right price.

> **Instead of dropping the price, we dropped the agent.**

As Geoff told me, *"After I read your books, Neil, I was teaching agents the right way to sell."* I am always stunned that more consumers read my books than agents.

So together, we all decided: Instead of dropping the price, we dropped the agent.

We interviewed another agent who was more optimistic. She had read my books. She knew how to negotiate. Plus, she was coached by Australia's best real estate coach, Michael Kies. This new agent was *not* from Geoff's immediate area. This meant that, unlike local agents, this "foreign agent" was not price prejudiced.

Within weeks of changing agents, Geoff's home sold for $4.95 million PLUS some generous terms.

Geoff Lane, as I had surmised, was not greedy.

✓ DON'T DECREASE, INCREASE THE PRICE (Maybe).

"If I struggle to sell something, I mark it up, not down.
Works all the time."

Michael Bloomberg. New York billionaire

Unless you have studied negotiation, you may think this idea is ridiculous. It's not. It has great merit. And it often leads to a faster sale – at a better price!

Instead of dropping the price – as agents urge – it's often better to increase the price. I have often used this strategy myself. In the 1970s, I owned a home in Mona Street, Auburn. The price was $50,000 (the equivalent of $500,000 today). After six weeks, the home hadn't sold.

It's often accepted that there are only two reasons a home does not sell: Either the price is too high, or the agent is incompetent. Of course, sellers always blame the agent, and agents always blame the sellers.

I dropped the agent and increased the price. From $50,000 I upped it to $55,000. I then placed an ad for private sale (no agents). It sold the next weekend for $55,000 – with no commission.

More recently – in around 2022 – a husband and wife contacted me. Their home had been for sale for a year. All they had were low offers. I was astonished. It was a beautiful home on 8 acres. It resembled a movie star's mansion. When I showed photographs to people and asked them to estimate the price, answers ranged from five million dollars to $25 million. The home was a couple of hours from Melbourne. Local agents listed it at "$1.6 million to $1.8 million". My first thought was: "Why so cheap?"

The main reason was the attitude – the prejudice – of the local agents. As they often told the owners, *"No home in this area has sold for more than $2 million."* That sort of thinking shows a complete lack of initiative. It's thinking that prevents progress. Just because something has never been done it doesn't mean it can't be done.

My advice was to hire an out-of-area agent and increase the price to $2.8 million. Naturally, the owners agreed.

Well, didn't that cause a flurry among so-called "interested buyers". The first thing most asked was: *"Why has the price risen a million dollars?"* The reply was, *"Because the owners realised they were asking too little. The home has a replacement value of almost $5 million plus the value of the land. It should be offered for at least $5 million."*

> If you don't accept a low offer, you still own a beautiful home.

Within a week, someone offered $2 million. A few weeks later, the offers reached $2.4 million. The owners said no. They eventually decided to hold their beautiful home.

And here's the best part – as I often tell owners of beautiful homes: If you don't accept a low offer, you still own a beautiful home.

✓ ALLOW FOR GO-WRONGS

When selling a home, things go wrong. Minor disappointments are part of the process. Expect them and don't get upset. Try to avoid major go-wrongs, however, the worst of which is buyers reneging after negotiations. Remember this rule: Nothing in real estate is 100 percent certain until it's legally confirmed.

Agents often say, "Buyers are liars." Some buyers use up your time, agree on a price and terms and then, later, change their minds or – worse – offer you a lower price as you are about to sign at the agreed price.

For this reason – and to protect yourself – never chase away all buyers until your home is "legally sold". Only start negotiations with serious buyers. The test of seriousness is whether they pay a large deposit as a show of good faith.

Make it a policy: NO MONEY, NO TALKIE.

✓ VULTURES CIRCLING

Beware of vultures – especially if your home is for sale for more than a few weeks. Other agents start circling. They have one motive – to entice you away from your current agent. They will appear ever-so-nice, so caring. Vultures are great pretenders. They will feign surprise that your home hasn't sold. They will often say, *"There's nothing wrong with the price."*

Sure, until you list with them.

The two biggest (worst) ways that vulture agents entice sellers from listed agents are:

"We've got a buyer for you!"

First, they will claim to "have a buyer". This buyer will be someone only known to this agent. A complicated story will follow – a sure sign of deception. If vulture agents are especially pushy, they may claim to know "several buyers who'd love this home". Their aim is to make you feel like you are missing out with your current agent.

> Vultures are great pretenders.

In almost all cases, when owners switch agents, their homes sell for lower – not higher – prices. Most sellers are better off staying loyal to their current agent.

So, here is the best way to test the sincerity of the vulture agents:

Tell them: *"We like our current agent because he/she will always do what's best for us. We mentioned that you contacted us saying you had a buyer who'd pay a higher price than our current agent can obtain. And so, our agent said if that's true, he'll charge us no commission, you can have it all. When do you want your buyer to inspect our home?"*

This is the "put up or shut up technique".

Silence will be the likely reply.

"The marketing is not good enough."

Second, they will claim the marketing is not good enough. As already proven, the claims that agents make about advertising are misleading to the point of fraudulent. I have rarely encountered a nicer couple than Edgar and Marion, a middle-aged couple selling their home in the Melbourne suburb of Glen Waverley. The home had unique features. It was a great example of a home that only suits buyers with similar taste. But, having been months on the market, Edgar and Marion were starting to panic.

Enter Miss Vulture – from an agency where unethical conduct is compulsory (all sellers are conned to pay $5,000 for a premium ad). Miss Vulture was adamant: They *needed* a premium ad. Being desperate to sell, Edgar paid $5,000. Nothing happened. Except, of course, that Miss Vulture got five thousand dollars of free publicity and more leads for herself.

Eventually, Edgar and Marion slashed the price and sold their home.

Here's how to handle the vulture agents: Get their promises in writing. And then, if they don't keep those promises, they must agree not to charge you. Demand what consumers get when they buy a toaster – a GUARANTEE.

✓ MYSTERY SHOP

If you want to know what buyers are being told about your home, mystery shop the agent.

But brace yourself.

The things some agents say about their clients and their listings are hard to believe.

As many sellers say, after mystery shopping their agent: "To hear an agent who expects us to pay thousands of dollars in commission denigrating our home feels like a knife in the back."

If you mystery shop an agent, be prepared for the anger you'll feel at the betrayal you discover.

And here's the worst part: If you have signed a "standard" Selling Agency Agreement, you will be stuck with an agent who is not acting in your best interests.

Oh sure, you can try and take legal action for "failure to uphold their fiduciary duty", but most sellers don't have the stomach for confrontation, never mind a legal fight.

Instead, their only choice is to "wait out" the period of the agreement and hire a better agent.

✓ IT'S THE SYSTEM THAT'S DISHONEST

Even honest agents cannot treat clients ethically if they are forced to use a dishonest system.

Every method used by agents involves placing the interests of agents ahead of the interests of clients. So, everything a typical agent says – as good as it sounds – must be treated with scepticism.

Here's a classic statement from the man who calls himself Australia's Number One Real Estate trainer.[101] It's from a video coaching a real estate salesperson. He shouts into his phone:

"What I want you to do now is go back to your existing vendors and get more marketing dollars. Why? Because you are going to use those marketing dollars to get more listings."

To hear this agent-cum-auctioneer training agents is to hear a barrage of selfishness.

It could be a coincidence but since this bloke burst on to the real estate scene as a trainer, the public distrust of agents has never been worse.

As of 2024, research shows 95 percent of people consider real estate agents untrustworthy.

✓ BEWARE OF "NICE AGENTS" OR "FRIENDS IN REAL ESTATE"

Harry Truman said, *"If you want a friend in Washington, get a dog."* The same applies in real estate.

The commissions in real estate are now so large that friendship is out of fashion. The first person who said: *"They'd sell their own mother for a buck,"* was probably referring to real estate agents.

Five words make us shudder: *"We know a nice agent."* Or *"A friend is an agent."*

Our immediate reaction to these words is: "You are 100 percent certain to be ripped off."

As my dodgy dad would giggle: *"You can't cheat your enemies; they don't trust. But your friends, they are so easy to cheat."* At his sixtieth birthday party, no one had known him more than a year. That's mostly because he'd cheated all his old friends. I was ashamed of him.

The real estate world is too dangerous for anyone to place friendship ahead of prudence. If you think that because you have a friend who's an agent or that you like an agent, you'll get fair treatment, think again. Do you really think that nice agent will remove nasty conditions just for you? Change their methods? Anger their bosses? No way.

There is only one way to know if an agent will treat you fairly: **Who has control?** If you have control, you're safe. But if that nice agent expects you to sign a document filled with nasty clauses, then that nice agent is not a nice agent. Evil is everywhere in real estate and there's nothing more dangerous than a friend who stands to pocket thousands of dollars from your trust.

Heed the words of the novelist Greg Iles: *"True evil has a face you know and a voice you trust."*

32 QUESTIONS
TO HELP YOU TRANSFER CONTROL FROM THE AGENT TO YOU
AKA
HOW TO BAFFLE STUPID AGENTS WITH COMMON SENSE

Most agents have three characteristics. They are greedy, they are lazy, and they are stupid.

The hardest characteristic for home sellers to comprehend is stupidity. Don't agents realise that the better they treat sellers, the more home sellers they will attract? Apparently not because there are very few truly smart agents. Well-intentioned perhaps; well-learned, rarely.

When you meet agents, especially those you feel you like, here are some questions, any of which may "shock them into some degree of sensibility".

Agents with a sense of decency who strive to be ethical will admit that what they witness in the industry does not sit well with them.

So, here are 32 questions to ask agents. Decent agents will answer frankly. If they weave or remind you of a politician, don't hire them.

> *1. How do you feel being one of the least trusted professions?*
>
> *2. Do you see things in real estate that make you feel uncomfortable?*
>
> *3. Is it true that many agents put their interests ahead of their clients' interests?*
>
> *4. Are you aware that many homes are undersold?*

5. *How often are properties undersold at auction? You may want to rephrase this question thus: How many times at auctions are winning bidders willing to pay more?*

6. *How often do you get calls from ads from buyers known to you?*

7. *Is a main reason for advertising to promote agents?*

8. *There are 195 countries in the world. Are you aware that Australia is the only country where sellers pay advertising money before their homes sell?* [102]

9. *In all other countries, all costs are included in the commission, which is payable when a home has sold. Did you know this?*

10. *Why must Australian sellers get such a raw deal?*

11. *Are you aware that most home sellers are uninsured for open inspections?*

12. *At an auction, the sellers' lowest price is called "the reserve". What do you agents call the buyers' highest price?* [103]

13. *Agents say auctions are transparent. Sure, the agents know the sellers' lowest price – and so, usually, do buyers. That's transparent. But the highest price the buyers will pay is concealed. Don't you think it's unfair that sellers must disclose their lowest price, but buyers don't? Surely, transparency should apply to everyone?*

14. *There are two bidders at an auction. One can pay up to $2 million. The other can pay up to $2.5 million. How can agents make sure the sellers receive $2.5 million?*

15. *When you are selling one house, do you meet buyers who have a home to sell?*

16. *If you expect us to pay for advertising, and our ads attract other sellers, and you list and sell their homes, do you give us commission from those sales? Or do you keep this money for yourself?*

17. Would you agree that agents ask sellers to pay thousands of dollars in advertising costs – and then ask other sellers in, say, the next street, to also pay thousands in advertising costs – and the same buyers respond to both advertising campaigns?

18. Why do you advertise every home? Surely, by advertising the most appealing homes you can attract every buyer in the area without wasting thousands of dollars of sellers' money. Supermarkets don't advertise every product. They just advertise specials to attract buyers for all products. Agents could do the same, surely?

19. Do you think it's unethical for agents to charge sellers for advertising their homes when the buyers for those homes are known to the agents?

20. Have you heard where two agents have a buyer for the same home – and yet the buyer given to the owners is from the agent who listed the home not the agent who finds the best paying buyer?

21. Can other salespeople in your office work on our home when you are unavailable?

22. Would you agree that most people who inspect open houses never buy those houses?

23. If you meet a buyer at an open house who loves our home and you must go to another open house, that buyer is left unattended and can look at other houses, is that right?

24. If a buyer likes our home, surely it is best to make the sale immediately rather than let the buyer inspect more homes – and find a similar one at a lower cost?

25. We insist that all people who inspect our home are identified and qualified. We don't want hordes of sticky-beaks. Is that okay by you?

26. Are you okay to show our home at a time to suit buyers instead of a time to suit you?

27. *Do you ever have buyers who make offers and say this is their best offer, and you pass this offer to the sellers and the sellers refuse and then the buyers increase their offer?*

28. *How does it make you feel when you, in good faith of course, tell sellers that you have an offer from buyers and it's the highest they are willing to pay; but then, as mentioned, they increase their offer?*

29. *How can you be sure buyers who want our home are making their best offer?* [104]

30. *Have you heard of Professor William Vickrey?* [105]

31. *Something puzzles us. Most agents claim they do what's best for their clients, but surely the answers to these questions prove that most agents do what's best for agents?*

32. *Would you be willing to work with our supporter, a friend with real estate knowledge and experience who knows how to ensure we control our interests?*

IMPORTANT AND OBVIOUS POINT: The best agents study relentlessly. They read every book on real estate they can find. They attend seminars and lectures and not just those presented for the benefit of agents, but those focused on client care. The best agents study negotiation. They do not refer to "conditioning" as negotiating. Good agents can obtain hundreds of thousands of dollars more for homes than typical agents. The best agents also know how to ensure buyers offer their best price. This is why the very best agents are worth more than the worst agents.

> **The best agents study negotiation.**

If a good agent charges one percent more than a bad agent (3 percent instead of 2 percent) and the good agent sells your home for 10 percent more, surely the good agent is worth an extra one percent.

And the good news is: With good agents you pay nothing until your home sells and you're happy.

HOW TO FIRE AN AGENT

The more the agent controls you, the harder they are to fire.[106]

"You should have read what you signed!" one agent in Sydney's Eastern Suburbs[107] allegedly yelled at a disgruntled elderly seller who received a bill for several thousand dollars when the agent couldn't sell his home for the price the agent originally quoted. The outraged seller – who, like many sellers, only listed his home with this agent because of the price the agent first quoted him – told the agent to "get lost" with his absurd advertising invoice.

A caveat was then placed on the home. All this stress, disappointment and wastage of thousands of dollars after signing up with this agent who calls himself "Australia's number one agent".

As I often say to sellers and buyers, I'd rather protect you than rescue you. Like we had to do with Frank and Jenny who sold their home in the Melbourne suburb of Kew.

Frank signed up with an agent (who also calls himself "Australia's number one agent").[108]

"We should have done our research before signing up," mused Frank. But Jenny had never liked this agent who she dubbed "the show pony". If only more "blokes" listened to their wives.[109]

When they found an agent who offered them the protection they needed and who had the skills (and intelligence) to get the best price, Frank rang the "show pony" agent to fire him. Not so fast, jeered the show pony. Frank discovered the meaning of "controlled listing". He was locked up with the show pony for four months.

Things got heated when Frank uttered a word that's a malediction to many agents, especially self-promoting self-titled "legends" and "superstars". That word was "Jenman". Frank explained how I had told him about the stupidity of selling by auction. I then helped Frank find an agent who was a superb negotiator and who offered risk-free protection conditions.[110] Unlike the show pony, this second agent does not control his sellers.

The agent exploded: *"There is no way I'll release you from the Listing Agreement. As for Neil Jenman, I'll have him charged with enticement."* Mm … Enticement is defined as: *"The quality of being attractive or tempting."* Not a crime.

> "... As for Neil Jenman, I'll have him charged with enticement."

But given that the show pony controlled him for four months, Frank was forced to do what many sellers do when determined to fire an agent. He waited it out.

When four months expired, Frank and Jenny – who felt like they were released from prison – were free to sign up with the good negotiator. Unlike what happens at auctions where homes are massively undersold, they soon sold their home for the highest market price. As Frank said, *"We waited four months and I reckon we got an extra $400,000."*

So, if an agent refuses to release you (as many do), then unless you want to engage in legal action, the only way to fire an agent is to "wait it out".[111]

Don't be afraid to stand up to agents, especially those doing wrong. Negotiating with agents is like negotiating with Russians;[112] toughness is essential. Take firm action to force agents to treat you well.

Another agent[113] refers to himself as "Australia's Number One Agent" (yes, another one to claim that title[114]). This bloke controls home sellers with dreadful deception and massive manipulation. He over-quotes the likely selling price of a home (by pushing auctions, the worst method of sale, as the best method). This makes the sellers keen to list with him.

But once the sellers sign up, this "number one agent in Australia" commences his conditioning control and manipulation. This bloke hits the sellers brutally and quickly. Within days, the price of his clients' homes plunge hundreds of thousands of dollars in value.

Here's an example of his modus operandi:[115]

The agent tells a retired couple their home is worth $750,000 to $800,000.[116]

Based on this (unknown to them) inflated quote, the couple sign up with this agent.

Two weeks later, the agent emails and says their home is now worth $650,000 to $700,000.[117]

Six days later, the agent emails again and says their home is now worth $620,000 to $680,000.[118]

At the same time, the agent gives the retired couple "market feedback" plus offers from buyers as low as $550,000.

In three weeks, this elderly couple see the value of their home drop from a high of $800,000 (when they signed up) to a low of $550,000. That's $250,000 down in three weeks. As one agent quipped about this "rock-star agent": *"Once you sign up with him, the value of your home drops a hundred thousand dollars a week."* [119]

And when your home starts off at $800,000, a drop of $100,000 per week is emotionally and financially sickening.

This agent doesn't care. All he cares about is making the sale. And promoting himself. And soon, he'll be off to teach thousands of other agents his "secrets".

But this bloke won't catch you, not now. Nor will any agent. Not after you've read this book. Not now that you know how to control agents instead of being controlled like most sellers.

Control – the most important word in real estate. Don't ever give control to an agent. Keep control – that's how to guarantee you get the best result. Always insist on being in control.

INSIST ON PROTECTION AND SUPPORT

Having read this far, if you feel you can trust me and my son Alec to help and protect you when you're selling a property, especially your family home, please consider contacting us at Jenman Support.

By "help" I mean everything from finding the right agent to supporting you through the entire sales campaign. In short, making sure that you, not the agent, controls the process. So you get the best result without being stung for needless costs.

We know agents in many areas of Australia who'll agree to our protection terms. When these agents accept our philosophy of placing clients' interests first, life is wonderful. A home seller calls us, gives their location and we immediately suggest an agent we trust.[120]

If we don't know a suitable agent, we try to find one for you. If we can't find a good agent, we can show you how to sell without an agent – and support you through the entire process. It's up to you: either you accept a typical agent, or you sell without an agent. I'd vote for the latter, for sure.

With around ten thousand people selling their homes every week in Australia, there are more sellers than we can ever help – at least with person-to-person support. We can, however, give every genuine seller complimentary information. And our website – jenman.com.au – has a wealth of helpful information, especially for subscribers to whom we send weekly alerts.

In many cases, we give away copies of our books, often with a collective retail value of more than a hundred dollars. As I keep saying, if you are a genuine and decent seller, we will do anything we can to support and help you. We ask for nothing other than your loyalty (stick with us) and to be treated as fairly as we treat you. Please.

POINT OF CONCERN

A few home sellers treat risk-free selling like a free lottery ticket. They take up hours of our time and make obsessive demands of the good agents we suggest, all of whom have agreed to our eight conditions to protect the sellers. It's not uncommon for these agents to rightly tell sellers: "Jenman puts more pressure on us to do the right thing than any sellers ever give us."

But some sellers seem to think: "Well, first we'll try the Jenman path and see if we can get a magical in-our-dreams price." If the miracle doesn't happen, they ditch us, fire the agent, then pay thousands of dollars to a typical agent. And sell for less. While I firmly believe in risk-free selling, it has never been my intention to hurt agents who are good enough to support ethics. Such as agreeing to do the right thing by the sellers – like covering the selling costs.

Therefore, I believe that if sellers choose a risk-free agent and decline the offers obtained by that agent and then, later, switch agents and sell for less than the first agent obtained, the sellers should, at least, reimburse the first agent for any expenses incurred on the sellers' behalf.

The worst type of rogue sellers is when the best agent gets the best price and then, later, after the sale is made, the sellers demand a commission cut.

Asking an agent for a discount after a sale is like asking a restaurant for a discount after a meal. If you don't like it, say something *before* you accept the sale (or eat the meal).

As one of Australia's best agents said: "Some people attracted by risk-free selling are terrible takers. We spend hours trying hard to get a few thousand dollars extra only to find that these sellers, instead of thanking us, demand a discount; and often long after they've agreed to the sale."

In over 50 years in the real estate industry, I can't recall a complaint from an honest consumer. Sure, we all encounter miserable people – the takers of the world – but, as my wife Reiden so often says:

Most consumers are wonderful. We need to be more careful to whom we give our time and support, that's all.

But both Reiden and I – and my son Alec (and my daughter Haley when she's not on maternity leave) – will always do the best we can humanly do to help honest and decent consumers. Allow me to repeat what's emotionally important to us: All we ask is that you treat us the same we treat you – with courtesy, respect and integrity. Thank you.

A BRIEF SUMMARY OF
HOW TO CONTROL REAL ESTATE AGENTS

As this book was nearing completion, we received this story/review from Geoff Lane of Sydney, one of the home sellers mentioned in the book.

It's a fine summary of what it means to sell when the home seller, not the agent, is in control.

HOW I SOLD
FOR AN EXTRA $700,000
WHILE MY NEXT-DOOR NEIGHBOUR
UNDERSOLD BY ABOUT $500,000.

by

Geoff Lane

In the real estate world, there can be many truisms but really, one simple fact. If you are selling your home without the advice of Jenman Support then, almost certainly, you are losing hard-earned money. A lot of it. A quick read of this experience will provide just one example of how a fully protected sale as advised by Jenman Support ensured the best price for a home, compared with a quick auction that unloaded another home too cheaply.

1. I list my home with a recommended agency who wants me to auction. I resist, preferring that the agent works hard at negotiating a best price sale. There's some marketing prepared, and a sale agreement offered which I insist includes a "No sale, No payment" clause. The agent offers the home to the market at a ridiculously inflated selling price estimate.

2. Weeks go by and interest declines, hastened by the agent successively lowering the asking price – eventually by over one million dollars below the initial sale estimate! The agent then fails to close a deal on a verbal offer of $4.5M, resorting to the suggestion of taking a $4.25M written

offer. "It's the market talking," he says. In absolute frustration, I terminate the sale at no cost to me. Remember, No sale, No payment – for anything.

3. I seek the advice of Neil Jenman personally who introduces me to an independent, out-of-area agent. Not intimidated by local-franchise, auction-agent comparisons and nonsensical "the market has declined" falsehoods, this new agent gets to work immediately, inviting buyers to individually tailored inspections and personal, honest negotiations. After a short campaign conducted with the full protection of the Jenman 8 Seller Protection Points Guarantee, the property sells for $4.95M, a full $700,000 more than the earlier lazy effort!

4. But this story doesn't end there! A mere 3 months later, after much presentation work, paint-jobs and an expensive styling effort, the larger, next-door neighbouring house goes to auction with a "big name" agency. "On the market" and bidding finishing at $4.9M ("the reserve"). The dressed-up, larger, well-appointed home sells for less than mine next door... in a rising market!

There's no doubt that buyer is laughing at the windfall of up to half a million dollars at least – the amount almost certainly lost by the vendor opting for a quick sale by auction, managed by a lazy process. A classic example of the typical failure of the auction system in which daily, homes are sold significantly under Best Price.

Neil Jenman has given his life to protecting homeowners and has become a friend through this process. We communicate often, observing failures of typical home auctions as conducted by too many agencies. The auction system provides lazy agents with free self-marketing, more client leads and quick commissions at the expense of a negotiated fair, strong price for a vendor's greatest asset. It is quantity over quality in selling. It is dodgy at best, corrupt in many cases. My many years observing real estate sales have shown me too many sad stories of serious financial loss.

Please, do not sell your home by auction. Contact Jenman Support. Get an honest, hard-working agent, receive the 8 Seller Protection Points that ensure you do not lose thousands of dollars from the value of your asset and that you get a guaranteed Best Price for your home.

****

AFTERWORD
The thin line between success and failure
by Neil Jenman

The factor that gives me the greatest feeling of success in my working life also gives me my greatest feeling of failure.

When people contact Jenman Support and use our services, I feel successful. Of all the roles I have had within real estate, nothing makes me happier than helping sellers achieve a better price with lower costs and less stress. As Alec tells people who ask him what he likes best about Jenman Support: *"The gratitude from people we protect and support."*

Imagine how it feels when sellers say: *"Neil, at my age (65) to get an extra $365,000 for our home – thanks to your support – makes a huge difference to our life."* Or the farmer who cancels his auction and sells for millions of dollars more than he would have sold at auction.

And the elderly retiree who sold two homes for such a great price that he donated the entire proceeds from one home – more than a million dollars – to charity.

What a positive difference to the lives of so many people. It makes me feel so successful.

But then come feelings of failure and frustration.

When thousands of sellers lose tens of thousands of dollars each, it makes me despondent.

What have I done wrong? Why did they not take my advice? They are underselling their homes by hundreds of thousands of dollars and forking out thousands of dollars in needless expenses.

The line between success and failure is thin. The difference between a great price and the best price can easily be thousands of dollars. One – selling too low and paying too much in needless costs – is failure.

The other – selling for the best price at the least cost – is success. Most sellers fail to get the best price (whether they know it or not). To me, that's failure.

The difference between failure and success comes down to two factors: Knowledge and control.

We wrote this book to give you the knowledge you need and the control you deserve. All we ask now is that you be fiercely determined to *keep* that control, to insist on protecting your own interests, especially the value of your home. With control, you'll avoid the failure suffered by most of Australia's home sellers. You will achieve the success you seek and deserve.

ADVICE TO AGENTS

Way back in 2007, a reporter[121] from the television show 60 Minutes described me as "one of the world's best salesmen". It was a reference to my life in a real estate office and my sales results.

The secret to any success I achieved was so simple, it's near embarrassing. *I cared about clients.* I placed clients' needs ahead of my own needs. After all, my clients were my sellers and they paid me.

This secret – caring for clients – was so powerful it made me the leading agent in my area within ten months of opening my agency. Ten years later, my sales and management seminars attracted agents from all over Australia – and the United States. I told them all how to do it: *Care for your clients.*

And don't just say it, *do it.* Don't just sprout platitudes, deliver incredible service. Offer what few agents offer – a Service Guarantee.[122]

The message I preached to thousands of agents for more than 25 years was always the same: Do what's best for your clients. Walk your talk.

While I may be embarrassed at the simplicity of my success system, I am not shy to say that looking after clients was good for me too. I achieved success never equalled in the world of Australian real estate training. I laugh at the twerps who've tried to follow me as they strive to attract agents by focusing on what's best for agents. Most are former failed agents – and who wants to follow a selfish loser? That's why you're doing poorly, fellas.

My message to all real estate agents is as simple now as it's always been: If you aspire to financial success, place your clients' interests ahead of your own. Stop acting like salespeople. Start helping people. Tell your clients the truth. You have no obligation to agents; they don't pay your commission.

Your duty is to the home sellers in your area.

If you study negotiation, you'll abandon most methods of most agents and you'll start getting the best prices for your sellers. If you offer risk-free selling, you'll attract more sellers. Word will spread. Believe it, being chronically short of listings, like most agents, won't apply to you.

When you place the interests of your clients ahead of your own interests, you'll have more clients than you'll ever be able to handle.

That's all I have got to say in this book for agents. Other than this: If you are genuinely interested in placing the interests of sellers ahead of your own interests, let us know. We'll be happy to test you – and see if your actions match your words. Our greatest challenge is finding more good ethical agents.

JOIN US AT JENMAN?

If you have enjoyed this book and you would like to consider helping us to support and protect real estate consumers, please contact us.

You can work from anywhere in Australia.

You will need:

Immense integrity and, hopefully, to have done (or be doing) something meaningful.

A genuine desire – preferably a passion – for protecting good and decent people.

A basic understanding of the real estate industry and how most agents operate.

To learn how to protect and support real estate consumers, we will suggest how you can acquire the necessary knowledge.

To be available at rostered days and hours to receive calls or contact consumers who enquire.

You will receive:

Not much in terms of money (right now) but it should prove to be one of the most satisfying roles of your life.

If this feels okay to you, please consider applying to join us.

CONTACT REIDEN JENMAN on support@jenman.com.au

Thank you.

WORDS FROM A FEW SELLERS

Attributed: Google Reviews

Rohan Pigott
I can truthfully say that without the support from Neil and his team, we would have vastly undersold our family home.

Angela and Graeme Martin
Not only has he written great guides to buying and selling real estate, but he lives and breathes what he writes about and backs it up with a personal approach. We highly recommend anyone contemplating a real estate transaction to contact Neil Jenman.

Ed Murphy
I have long held that Neil Jenman is the ONLY source of good, impartial advice in the real estate market. Jenman Support is a valuable resource for sellers.

Pamela Thrift-Mulholland
Jenman Real Estate Support have assisted my husband and I twice to locate ethical agents, who were able to achieve an excellent price for our properties on both occasions, without any hassles at all.

Jason M
I sold my house at a very pleasant price with unimaginable ease. Thank you Mr. Jenman and all your staff for your genuine and ongoing concern for the welfare of the individual undertaking the mammoth task of selling their very often beloved home.

Louise Casey
I have watched this gentleman, Neil Jenman and later, his son, Alec, for a couple of decades waiting for the day when I may need an effective reliable agent with integrity. In the meantime, I have inadvertently learned so much about what I can do to sell my home successfully, from the wisdom and generosity of spirit in sharing this valuable wisdom to homeowners and home buyers, of Neil and Alec Jenman. If you want to know how to sell or buy a home the right way, I highly recommend this family-run business.

Peter
I first came across the work of Neil over 30 years ago. He has been a beacon of light for so many wishing to get the best outcome for their property purchase whether as buyer, seller or investor.

Kristine Colliver
My recommendation to future sellers and buyers is to ONLY deal with Jenman Real Estate Support. They will guide you and support you through the process, with only your best interests at heart.

CL Family
On one of my properties recently, following Neil's advice we achieved a price 10% higher than what the other agents were telling me. Neil's advice works. I can't recommend him highly enough.

James Turton

Profound thanks for the incredible efforts that Neil Jenman went to personally to ensure the highest possible selling price for my family home.

You could do no better in finding a seller's advocate to assist in negotiating the harrowing and confusing maze that is the Australian real estate industry.

Robert Taylor

The support office has helped us find an agent with integrity and strong ethics. This agent is trying very hard to achieve a positive outcome for us and has left no stone unturned.

Adrian Sheehy

I have just sold my house. The biggest mistake I made was not to consult with Neil or his staff before engaging a real estate agent.

Cal Chikwendu

If anyone is considering selling their house, we would highly recommend you speak to Neil Jenman – he is the real deal, he will help demystify the process of selling your house in a genuine and compassionate way. And he'll give you the confidence to sell your own home if that's what you want to do. If you don't – he knows the ethical, decent and good real estate people. He'll work with you to work with them! Neil will support you all the way, so the money goes in your pocket instead of someone else's – not even in his pocket.

Ingrid Vogelzang

What more can one possibly ask than step-by-step support through the entire journey.

Stuart Bell

Call Neil and team and ask for an agent recommendation in your area to talk to before signing anything.

Michael Ukhoff

Call Jenman Support and let them do the hard work. After all it will cost you nothing except peace of mind.

Susan Tselepis

Their support throughout the sale process was invaluable and certainly helped lower the stress levels associated with such a big (and life changing) decision involved in selling my home. Wouldn't even consider selling in the future without the backup of the Jenman team!

Frank Facciolo

Jenman Support offers the service home sellers have long needed. If every seller knew what they do, every seller would contact them. I hope that day comes. I am spreading the word about these wonderful people and how hard they fight to help consumers. Thank you, Neil, and Alec.

Ceridwen Dumergue

Five stars isn't nearly enough to describe the service we have received from Neil Jenman. This is a man who genuinely cares about the welfare of honest and kind consumers.

Sajee Wijesena
I felt like I was truly cared for like a family member the whole way. I would not hesitate to recommend Jenman Support to anyone who wishes to be protected and obtain the best price for their home.

Astra Temple
I think Neil Jenman is an amazing man who has done so much good and helped so many ordinary people navigate in the real estate 'minefield' he deserves a bucket load of medals. His books are an enormous help and so easy to read and understand, also the seminars of his that I attended years ago were an absolute godsend at the time and have definitely continued to be a great help to me today. I highly recommend him and the Jenman group/support to everyone.

Vancho Bonevski
I would highly recommend Neil Jenman and his group to anyone thinking of selling real estate, whether it's your home or investment.

Merv Kiley
A conversation with Neil Jenman is a life-changing experience. Neil's passion, sincerity and insights are game changing and provided me with the opportunity to reconsider one of the biggest of life's decisions – whether to offload a much-loved property or not.

Tom Karamzalis
What Neil's guy did in a month, the others could not do in a year. If you are looking for someone to help you find a real estate agent in your local area, Neil Jenman is your man!

Craig McGill
Look, this will be simple: do NOT *EVER* contemplate selling your home without first contacting Jenman. He will provide you FREE support and advice to help you sell your home for the best price and, best of all, advise you how to avoid being ripped off, scammed and cheated. There's no argument: call his people. There's no sell, no cost, no hidden agenda – just free advice and free publications. So, what's the catch? Well, I've been getting advice from him for over a decade and there isn't any!

Julie Colman
If you want someone who will not take advantage of your naivety or lack of knowledge in the minefield of real estate, I whole-heartedly recommend you make contact with Jenman Support. I cannot thank them enough! Please do not hesitate to contact Jenman Support for advice – YES FREE advice – NO obligation FREE advice!

Sean Lacey
Alec is a top bloke, just like his dad. Alec was very helpful and diligent; I have no hesitations in recommending Jenman Support to anyone.

Steven Paul
A great sales result was achieved when selling an investment property by using the agent referred by JENMAN SUPPORT. It was great to know I always had professional support a phone call away if I needed it. Highly recommend the Jenman System and Jenman Support!

Alix Simpson

When I wished to sell our house, I contacted Jenman Real Estate online; unfortunately, there wasn't a Jenman agent in my area, but you assisted me every step of the way allowing me to sell privately which helped me to save the whole commission. I couldn't have done it without your help; you gave me the courage to sell our house myself.

Katrina Barker

Neil and his team have been exceptional. They have helped us with a bad agent and found us a good agent. They have also made us feel at ease about the selling process. It can be quite daunting, but Neil and his team have given us peace of mind.

ACKNOWLEDGEMENTS

Harold Edgar Lanyon was my grandfather. He was born in 1894. Within weeks of the outbreak of the First World War, Harold enlisted in the AIF. He turned 21 at Gallipoli. He was wounded and stretchered to a hospital ship. When he recovered, he rejoined the fighting. He was overseas almost five years.

Upon his return, Harold bought land in the Sydney suburb of Eastwood, built a home, became a surveyor, married, and raised four children.

His eldest child was my mother, Ruth Joan Jenman (nee Lanyon).

I knew my grandfather well. He had courage and integrity. I admired him. I still own letters he wrote from that awful war in which 61,687 Australians died and another 150,000 were wounded.

There is a word peppered throughout my grandfather's letters. It's a word rarely used nowadays.

That word is "shirker". It described cowards.

Recently I was speaking with an agent. He had once been one of my supporters. But, like many agents, he couldn't resist "the dark side". Our conversation grew heated until, in a fit of pique, he said: *"Why do you keep going, Neil? Why don't you live on your farm and forget real estate?"*

Because I am not a shirker; that's why.

The twenty-first century is different from my grandfather's days when the word "duty" was common.

I feel that qualities such as courage, loyalty and honour are not common now. It seems more common to focus on helping oneself before helping others. Shirkers are commonplace in the twenty-first century.

So, to those people who've stuck with me over the years (including, I am pleased to say, a growing number of agents), thank you. I couldn't continue without you.

My wife Reiden deserves my greatest thanks, not just for her decades of love and loyalty but for tolerating my obsession with trying to bring ethics into real estate – a task that often leaves me flat and forlorn.

Her smile always lifts my spirits. Reiden is the nicest person I have ever known.

To my son Alec, who has worked with me since leaving school in 2019, thank you for your commitment. Your care for others makes me proud. I have never said this, but you remind me of your great-grandfather, Harold Edgar Lanyon. And your maternal grandfather Maxwell Maurice McKay. They'd be proud to see you today.

To those who've worked with me for years such as our wonderful secretary, Debbie Matthews, I'm so grateful.

And, Australia's most truly successful agent, Michael Kies. Today he helps us find good agents. He performs a tough task without complaint. I have never had a better friend than Michael Kies.

I often think of all those who helped me in my real estate office – from Ivan Whitla to Don Ferguson and Reg O'Brien, three bank managers who were like father figures; right through to "Mustafa the Turk" at the Auburn café who fed me so late so many nights. He often said I was "the hardest working Aussie he'd met". Well, I don't think I've worked as hard as so many migrants.

Thank you for your custom, your friendship and, most of all, your great company.

All the sellers and buyers who made my real estate agency so successful, I still think of you with much fondness. A few years ago, while at the MCG with my wife, I got a text from a man and his wife who bought a home from me in 1989. They were splitting up. They said, *"The only thing we still agree on is that we both trust Neil Jenman."* That, to me, is success.

The best working days of my life have been when I've helped sellers and buyers.

To all who read my books and subscribe to the Jenman website, thank you sincerely. I would not persevere if I didn't have what makes me most proud – your unequivocal support.

Finally, thank you to all those people of Baralaba who've welcomed me home.

SOURCE NOTES

1. Reg Baglow Real Estate, Yeppoon.
2. Paul Pace – formerly from Penrith, now Paul Pace Country (NSW).
3. Bill Austin – First National Real Estate Homeway, Castle Hill.
4. Ben Hecht – Park Real Estate. Formerly Boronia, Victoria. Last sighted, Maroochydore, QLD.
5. This man – whose name I refuse to have in my book – has fleeced untold decent people whose only "sin" was ignorance or stupidity. But a person's intelligence (or lack thereof) is not justification to steal as this bloke does. And that's just real estate. When it comes to other dealings, he's just as wicked. Only those who don't know him or those as evil as him could possibly support him. Tragically, ignorance and evil seem ubiquitous in today's world. Be careful. Don't ever think this bloke will be your friend. He knows the great rule of crooks: *"You can't fleece your enemies because they don't trust you. So, fleece those who trust you – your friends."*
6. Selling Agency Agreements are legally binding contracts. They are designed by lawyers at the behest of agents with the main intention of protecting the agents. And they sure do exactly that. Agents tend to play down these "listing agreements" as standard. They say that "everyone signs them". They say the agreements are "approved by the real estate institute". That's the same as a hitman being approved by the mafia. Do not sign any agreement with any agent until you have deleted all the nasty clauses designed to control (and screw) you.
7. "Don't Sign Anything" is also the title of a book I wrote in 2002. Its advice is even more applicable today. Many readers say it's my best book. To purchase, go to jenman.com.au.
8. Always remember that the agreement agents ask you to sign are legally enforceable contracts which have been designed by lawyers paid by those representing agents. If that doesn't make you careful, this author despairs. What more can I do?!
9. My office, which I opened on February 18, 1984 was originally located at 84b Auburn Road Auburn, and later it was located at 11 Beatrice Street, Auburn.
10. If you can't find a good agent and you'd like to consider selling without an agent, we have a few hundred copies of a book on how to sell without agents. To receive a copy (provided they are still in stock), call 1800 1800 18 or email the author on support@jenman.com.au.
11. Coronis Realty – circa 1999.
12. From the poem 'Your Heart' by Leonard Cohen (1934–2016).
13. See Point 8 above.
14. *The Real Estate Office Manual* by Alan Fleming. Published by the Real Estate Institute of Australia Ltd, Canberra, with which are affiliated the Real Estate Institutes of New South Wales, Victoria, Queensland, South Australia, Western Australia, Tasmania, Northern Territory and the ACT. ISBN: 0909784620.

15. This technique of using sellers' money to create more listing leads is widely taught to agents. The man who likes to think of himself as Australia's top real estate trainer teaches the following to agents: *"What I want you to do is go back to your existing sellers and get more marketing dollars. Why? Because you're going to use those dollars to create more listings."* Tom Panos – in a video leaked to author by an agent appalled at what she was being taught by Panos.

16. MLS stands for Multiple Listing Services. Cooperating real estate agents share information about their individual listings. Any agent in the MLS can bring buyers to the listed home. The selling agents and agents who find buyers share the commission.

17. In 1962, US President John F Kennedy announced four basic rights for consumers: 1) the right to safety; 2) the right to be informed; 3) the right to choose; and 4) the right to redress. None of these rights are available to Australia's real estate consumers. Unless demanded.

18. Section 45A of the Trade Practices Act (amended 1977). Collusive behaviour is detrimental to the economy and consumers and is prohibited under the longstanding cartel provisions and the new criminal cartel provisions in Part IV of the TPA (Trade Practices Act of 1974). Regulation Impact Statement on Anti-competitive Price Signalling. Despite these laws, many agents – especially in regional centres (such as Forster in NSW) – show strong signs of colluding to keep commissions high. This is most noticeable when most of the agents in an area seem to be charging the same (higher than average – 2%) rate of commission and refuse to discount.

19. The major websites don't want to upset agents, so they do not allow (BAN) advertising from private sellers. Fortunately, like many dodgy people, they think their wealth means they're smart. There are many ways to circumvent their selfish and childish bans. There are also many other ways that you can attract the same (or better) buyers without the major websites. As I write these source notes, I am planning another book: If you can't find a good agent, YOU ARE MUCH BETTER OFF SELLING WITHOUT AN AGENT. I show readers how to do it, gladly and at no charge. Either when the book is published or beforehand – just email the author on support@jenman.com.au and let us know a time (or range of times) when it's convenient for you to speak with me or Alec – by phone or zoom.

20. Despite the massive misinformation promoted by the real estate industry and those with financial ties to the industry, my 50+ years of experience has revealed one sure fact: The best way to sell a home is with an agent who's a great negotiator. Unfortunately, at least 90% of agents know nothing – and I mean zilch, nada, لا شيء, rien, 没有什么 – about negotiation. Back in 2019, this author researched one hundred agents. The results were disgraceful. Not one agent had read one book on the topic of negotiation. Nor had any agent done a course on negotiation, at least outside the real estate industry. Conditioning sellers down in price, bullying sellers to accept absurdly low offers, or going backwards and forwards with offers to and from buyers and sellers is not negotiating; it's messaging. My experience has revealed – on scores of occasions – that provided the sellers know a little about negotiation or, better still, enlist the support of a genuinely good negotiator, they will achieve a much better selling price than typical agents. The industry's claim that agents are "experienced negotiators and can therefore sell homes for more money" is utter nonsense. This author can provide countless examples of homeowners who sold their homes without agents for much higher prices than they were quoted by agents. So, if you

do it right (find a supporter) not only will you almost certainly sell for a higher price, but your commission costs will also be the same as what most agents know about negotiating – nothing. The author's mate James Vonhoff is a better negotiator than any of the agents in his service area. And he's a humble (but brilliant) electrician. As well as being a man of decency and fine character.

21. 88 Reasons Why You Must Never Sell Your Home at Auction by Neil Jenman. Published March 2022 by Authors First, 25/7 Anella Avenue, Castle Hill, NSW 2154, Australia. National Library of Australia, Cataloguing-in-Publication entry: - Jenman. Neil. ISBN 9780958651790. RRP $14.95 plus $5 p/h from jenman.com.au or available at booktopia.com.au.

22. As there is no specific mandate that agents must provide home sellers with a guarantee, home sellers need to **demand a guarantee**. Just decide what you want, write it out and ask the agent to agree by signing your guarantee. Oh dear, thinks the agent, things are already looking a bit different. Suddenly, agents who are used to getting sellers to sign documents that effectively strip sellers of their rights and lock sellers in to harsh and unconscionable contracts with the sole purpose of controlling the sellers are now, wait for it, being controlled by the sellers. Seriously, good agents – or those who want your business badly enough to put their egos aside – will gladly give you a guarantee. At Jenman Support we will never pass on the details of any sellers unless the agents first sign off with us on what we call our 8 Protection Points. Essentially, these 8 points can be summed up in one sentence of nine words: The agent is not allowed to rip off the sellers. If you'd like a copy of these protection conditions or you'd like to see a copy of a Home Sellers' Protection Guarantee *that agents must sign before sellers sign*, email the author on support@jenman.com.au.

23. Lack of experience is one of the main reasons sellers get such a raw deal and why they lose so much money. The agents, however, have plenty of experience and you, the homeowner, has plenty of money. So, for your sake, please remember what can happen according to a well-known saying that applies in such situations: "When a person with money (you) meets a person with experience (agents), the person with the money is going to get some money and the person with the money is going to get some experience." Don't let such a cheeky but true quote apply to you. Get some knowledge from this book and, if you so wish, enlist the author's help to find and control an agent.

24. It's amazing how often this technique works. But you must use it! Don't be shy. It's an idea that, in this author's experience, succeeds in about 80 percent of cases. What this means is that you virtually get the commission for free. After all, if you were about to accept an offer of, say, $2.5 million (on which the commission at 2% is $50,000) instead you say to the agent: "Okay, we will accept this offer provided that $2.5 million is the amount we get net after paying your commission." It's a great idea; be sure to use it. If you prefer, say Neil Jenman suggested it. I don't mind you "throwing me under the bus" with this idea. What I mind is you paying commission that you did not have to pay. Let me know what happens. Your success makes my writing worthwhile.

25. Lizard Island.

26. One of the biggest signs of a dodgy agent is the inclusion of seemingly small but harmless fees – such as an "administration fee – $99". There is no such thing. Agents do not have an administrator to whom they pay $99 on each sale. Those little fees are far from harmless. They are a huge red flag that you are going to be ripped off. Behind closed

doors agents often scheme ways to fleece extra money from naïve and inexperienced home sellers, few of whom ever quibble about a hundred here or $75 there. From an agent's perspective, they say to themselves: "If we can get an extra $100 per sale and we are averaging 20 sales a month that's an extra $24,000 a year. In a decade that's almost a quarter of a million dollars for one teeny, little fee that most sellers are too inexperienced to notice or too shy to mention." Small fees are not small fees, they are BIG CLUES that you are dealing with a dodgy agent. Remember the Indian proverb: "A thief is a thief whether he steals a diamond or a cucumber." Agents who rip you off with little innocuous fees revealed at the start will later rip you off big time – count on it. No, better still, don't hire such agents.

27. For 30 years, I have regularly asked recent buyers how much more they were willing to pay for a home they just bought. On average nine out of ten buyers are willing to pay more. When asked, *"Why didn't you pay more?"* the usual reply is: *"We didn't have to."* Many times, it happens like this: Buyers make an offer – usually below the price they're willing to pay. The agent gets excited and tells the owners that this is a great offer, and it should be accepted. Many sellers accept, especially if the offer is at or slightly above their lowest agreed price.

You see, once an offer is accepted – once a seller says yes – the work for the agent stops. The commission is then certain. This is why most sales happen when sellers say yes, not when buyers say, "No more". Most homes are sold at – or slightly above – the sellers' lowest price. They are rarely sold at the Buyers' Highest Price.

28. Tom Panos.

29. *The Real Estate Office Manual.* Published by the Real Estate Institute of Australia. ISBN: 0909784620.

30. In an infamous 2003 television interview with New Zealand journalist Kim Hill, renowned Australian/British journalist John Pilger exposed Hill's ignorance on the topic being discussed – the Iraq War. Pilger, who effectively humiliated Hill, told her: "You waste my time because you have not prepared for this interview. This interview frankly is a disgrace." In a fit of petulance, Kim Hill appeared to throw Pilger's book across her desk. Pilger implored Hill – and the message was clearly intended for every viewer: **"Read! Just read. It takes time."** Yes, it sure does. But reading makes an enormous difference in life – both financially and personally.

31. Real Estate Institute of New South Wales – Northern division. Topic of this course – which ensures that agents keep their licence – is: "How to Protect Your Commission". There is no topic called "How to Protect Your Sellers from Paying Excess Commission".

32. As of 2024, we will not offer our books free to agents. When we send complimentary copies of this author's books to consumers, 90 percent reply with appreciation. It's the opposite with agents: Ninety per cent of agents never acknowledge a complimentary book. No more. If agents wish to read a Jenman book, they can do what millions of consumers have done or do – pay.

33. In recent years, New Zealand agents have started to emulate Australian agents. Many are gleefully embracing the VPA scams. Although the commission percentage in NZ is commonly twice as high as in Australia, it seems that 3.95 percent is not enough for many Kiwi agents.

34. Rohan Pigott, Mosman, NSW. After interviewing several agents in Mosman (one of Sydney's most exclusive suburbs), Rohan soon realised the absurdity (and chutzpah) of agents expecting sellers to pay tens of thousands of dollars for marketing expenses. One agent even quoted $50,000 in marketing, saying it was "essential". Rohan found an agent (from a nearby area) who sold her late-father's home for millions of dollars more than many agents estimated. Rohan and her sister, Swinder, did not risk a cent of their family's money on upfront expenses. Both these wise women should be an example to all home sellers. If you stand firm, the agents will either accept your terms or reject them – in which case you find a better agent. Either way, you control the sale of your home – as you should.

35. OPM – Other People's Money. A common saying in the real estate world. Whether investing in real estate or fleecing naïve home sellers, industry insiders think it's really clever to "use OPM".

36. As well as being too lazy to follow up prospects, most salespeople are too scared. They shirk one of the most important aspects of successful selling – following up prospects. If you agree to give an agent money to advertise to find prospective buyers for your home, you are encouraging that agent to be lazy and cowardly. You are rewarding them for their laziness. According to author and management consultant Michael LeBouef, the Greatest Management Principle in the world (famously known as GMP) is: *"What gets rewarded gets done."* Don't reward agents by paying them to be lazy and cowardly. Tell agents to follow up all current and past prospects rather than attempting to get you to pay to advertise to attract the same prospects.

37. The television program *Columbo* starring Peter Falk originally aired on NBC from 1971–1978. The character, Columbo, was a blue-collar Los Angeles detective whose bumbling and inept exterior disguised a razor-sharp intellect. One of his legendary techniques was to leave a room, only to return a few seconds later, saying: "Just one more thing," prior to asking a shrewd question that unnerved or exposed a suspect. Columbo could have used the "just one more thing" technique to expose the massive deception and hypocrisy of Australian real estate agents. For example: "Just one more thing: If you say I need to give you money to advertise to find a buyer for my home, why do I need you? Surely, I could advertise and find my own buyer?" OR: "Just one more thing: If you are confident you can sell our home for the full price of $3 million but you later ask us to sell for less than you quote, do you still charge us the full commission?" OR this question with an agent who's pushing public auction as the best way to get the best price: "Just one more thing: If you say that auctions get us the best price, why do you keep asking us for our lowest price? Why don't you discover the highest price that buyers will pay for our home?"

38. Although agents claim to know buyers that are not known to other agents, that's largely nonsense. Generally, all the active agents know all the active buyers in an area. Therefore, sellers should never choose the agent who claims to have "more buyers". Instead, sellers should list with the agents who are more readily available (such as after-hours and weekends) and, most important, agents who are more skilled in negotiation. The better an agent can negotiate, the better the price they'll obtain for your home.

39. Profiles for most areas are available online. In seconds, you should be able to discover how many homes are sold in your area each year. For example, in the Sydney suburb of Castle Hill there were 350 homes sold in one year (2023). Source: propertyvalue.com.au.

According to YellowPages.com.au, there are 160 agents servicing the Sydney Hills. One agent (Harcourts, Baulkham Hills) boasted at spending an average of $85,000 a month (more than $1 million a year) from property sellers with the VPA scheme (as told to author by Australia's best real estate trainer, Michael Kies). That real estate agency went broke. Just be sure that no agents make you broke through the VPA scheme of paying needless marketing costs.

40. realesate.com.au.

41. Such as domain.com.au – although less "traffic", Alec Jenman agrees with many agents and consumers that Domain is the better website. It has a host of excellent and exclusive features. And no, it is not necessary to advertise on many websites. Genuine buyers visit multiple websites. If a home is advertised on multiple websites, the buyers will think: "Gee, this home is advertised everywhere." Remember, protect the value of your home. Over-exposure damages the value of your home. And the cheaper the price, the easier it is to sell your home (and the sooner the agents get paid). As many agents (and buyers) are well aware: "The properties that are widely advertised are often the least desirable (the rejects). The best homes don't need to be mass-advertised."

42. Based on calculations from figures released by two of Australia's most widely visited property sites: realestate.com.au and domain.com.au.

43. QF635.

44. realestate.com.au.

45. In the Melbourne suburb of Northcote.

46. McGrath Estate Agents, 318 High Street, Northcote.

47. This executive was proud to tell the agent: "I work in the online real estate marketing business, and I know that you can get the same result for a $50 ad as you'd get for one of those "premium ads" that cost thousands of dollars."

48. Told to author during flight.

49. Core Realty, 284 La Trobe Street, Melbourne.

50. realestate.com.au.

51. Home in Rockhampton sold through McGrath.

52. Homes sold off-market (without massive advertising) are setting price records in their respective suburbs and categories. Only the most incompetent and/or dishonest agents demand advertising be paid by all their sellers. Agents are so enraptured with promoting themselves with sellers' money that many agents (the most stupid and egotistical) refuse to list a property unless the sellers pay (or agree to pay) thousands of dollars in (needless) advertising costs. Yes, some agents will give up a commission of $50,000 if they can't get $5,000 to promote themselves. Nuts, to be sure. But who ever said agents were astute businesspeople? Stupidity is a common characteristic among real estate agents.

53. One of my favourite sayings (by Benjamin Franklin) is: *"Laziness moves so slowly that poverty soon overtakes it."* Thousands of home sellers collectively lost hundreds of millions of dollars because of lazy agents. Lazy agents are those who are too lazy to study their craft, especially by focusing on benefits for clients. Lazy agents are also those who'd rather spend sellers' money advertising than spend their own time and effort following

up home buyers already known to those agents. Lazy agents definitely make sellers poorer.

54. Blaise Pascal (1623–1662). French mathematician, physicist, inventor, philosopher and writer.

55. Ask an agent: *"Can you please give us some examples of your negotiation skills, specifically how you can be sure you sell homes for the highest price that interested buyers are willing to pay?"* If you are not impressed, do not hire the agent. If you are not impressed with every agent to whom you put this question, maybe you should consider selling your home without an agent. Any home seller who has read the 42 Rules of Real Estate Negotiation will know far more about how to get the highest market price for their home than most agents will know. Only hire agents who have impressed you with their knowledge of negotiation – and maybe, also, specific examples of how their skill (not the real estate boom) has been responsible for achieving many record high prices.

56. *Relax and Sell More Real Estate* by Graham White 1986. Published by Team Training Sydney. ISBN 0 947075 00 3. Chapter 17, "Open For Inspections", page 135 *"If it is a property that pulls well, and we are meeting a lot of new people, then the worst thing we can do is sell it."*

57. James Packham of Harcourts Packham in Marion, SA. Agent training video. Circa 2019.

58. There are multiple examples of the danger of open inspections. One of the worst came to the attention of this author while writing this book. A 23-year-old woman, Celeste Mano, was murdered in a home in Umbria Road, Mernda, a north-eastern Melbourne suburb. Her killer, described as a "monstrous stalker", was "assisted by a floorplan", obviously sourced online or from an inspection where lookers are barely identified.

59. The New South Wales Department of Fair Trading releases a monthly list of the most complained about businesses. Agents often represent more than half of all complaints.

60. Pseudonym.

61. Without wanting to turn this book into an advertising campaign for Jenman Support, home sellers can get massive support by visiting the Jenman website (jenman.com.au) or by calling 1800 1800 18. Of course, with approximately 10,000 people selling their homes each week, we can't help everyone (at least not with personal one-on-one support), but we will always do our best to help honest and decent home sellers and buyers. Other than books and appearing as an expert witness, we rarely charge consumers. We are passionate about offering our services at NO EXTRA COST to consumers.

62. Obtain a copy of the booklet: Adding Extra Sparkles to Your Home. Available by calling 1800 1800 18 or email support@jenman.com.au.

63. Lucius Annaeus Seneca the Younger, usually known as Seneca, was a Stoic philosopher of Ancient Rome, a statesman, dramatist and satirist from the post-Augustan age of Latin literature. Born: Córdoba, Spain. Died: 65 AD, Rome, Italy. Source: from Wikipedia.

64. *Relax and Sell More Real Estate* by Graham White 1986. Published by Team Training Sydney. ISBN 0 947075 00 3.

65. Agent formerly with Biggin & Scott, Richmond, Victoria, to authors, Neil and Alec Jenman, in recorded interview in January 2020.

66. Ibid.
67. David Murphy Residential, 40 Cabramatta Road, Mosman. As well as being caught in this manner, Murphy was also caught (through mystery shopping) under-quoting the price of the sellers' home to prospective buyers. Murphy originally told the sellers (prior to listing) that they could sell for "$8 million to $10 million maybe more". Once listed, he was bringing offers in the six million range. He then denied quoting $10 million "maybe more". Fortunately, the owners followed Control Way 22 – 'Record the Agent' so Murphy was busted again. Murphy apparently makes the boast that no sellers have ever left him and obtained a better price with another agent. Another furphy from Murphy. After dismissing Murphy, the sellers later sold their home with another (out-of-area) agent for $600,000 more than the best price David Murphy had been able to obtain.
68. The book *Relax and Sell More Real Estate* by Graham White who was reportedly a senior real estate sales trainer for the LJ Hooker network. Chapter 8 – *"At the Auction"*, page 214. White writes: *"The vendors and purchasers. Remember, they are even more nervous than you are. It is your job to wander around and keep them nervous."* Published by Team Training Sydney. 1986. ISBN 947075 00 3.
69. It cannot be stressed often enough – auction is the absolute worst way to sell a home for the home sellers. But, as agents freely admit, auctions are the best way to sell homes at any price. I see it happen often. The auction agents are much better at convincing sellers to sell by auction than they are at getting the best prices for sellers. They can con well but they can't sell well. Any agent who says that public auction is the best way to get the best price is either a fool or a crook. Or both.
70. In my 20s, I discovered the big truth about Australia's real estate auctions: they are not about getting the best price, they are all about selling at any price. Sometimes I bought houses at auctions – usually abandoned derelicts sold by government departments – and re-sold them immediately for as much as treble the price. For example, 228 George Street, Erskineville. Bought for $16,800, re-sold immediately for $44,500.
71. Russell Haddan.
72. Ty Demirezen.
73. Scott Kim.
74. Tim Altass, Jeff Pickering, Arthur Conias, Danny Gurney, Stephen Smith.
75. Most sellers are intimidated by the sales process. They do not realise that they can delete or add many clauses to the agent's agreements. Remember, these Listing Agreements have been devised by lawyers to protect the interests of agents. They might be "standard" and it may be correct to state that "everybody signs them" or that they are "approved by the real estate institute" but that doesn't make them right or safe for the home sellers. If you sign an agent's selling agreement without, at the very least, deleting their nasty clauses, you will be under the complete control of the agent.
76. While writing this book I was asked to help a woman in her early 70s. Many years earlier, after she got divorced and her assets (including her former family home) were divided, she wanted to buy another home. Being a second-time home buyer, she was ineligible for the First Home Owner Grant. So, she asked her daughter if she could put the home in the daughter's name, thereby being able to fraudulently receive the First Home Owner Grant (an amount of just $15,000). The daughter agreed and the house was bought in

the daughter's name. Fast forward twenty years and the daughter is now claiming ownership of the home. After the mother racking up almost $800,000 in legal fees, it has been agreed that the home will be sold (for around $2 million) with the proceeds to be split evenly between the mother and the daughter. And so, as this woman approaches her mid-70s, she will have less than $200,000 in cash and no home. The consequences of cheating.

77. Homeowners would be shocked at how often their vacant (or vacated) homes are used by agents or their staff as "shagging pads". Given that as many as 60 percent of couples cheat on their partners and given that the first need of cheaters is a place in which to cheat, it's fairly obvious that real estate agents, with a cupboard full of keys to homes, find it hard to resist the temptation to "borrow" one of their owners' homes for an hour or so.

78. Visit jenman.com.au for many more tips on selling well. Or ask for personal assistance.

79. See Control Point 12.

80. As mentioned in Control Point 7, if you assure an agent that you'll "stick with" that agent (no legal obligation on your part, just a firm promise that, provided the agent does the right thing by you, you will not fire the agent at the end of the Listing Agreement term). Indeed, if the agent does well, you will re-sign for an extended period with the same agent and/or agree to stick with the agent until your home is sold. This will mean that the agent has no negative incentive to pressure you into accepting a lower price knowing that, unless you sell at any price, the agent will soon cease to be your agent. Look after the agent (if he or she deserves it) and the agent will likely look after you, especially a good and decent agent.

81. The exact figure is $576.92 per week; however, even with charging a modest interest rate you should receive at least $600 per week. A fair rate would be half a per cent (two basis points) below the average prevailing bank rate per year.

82. In the 1960s and 1970s, vendor finance was the only way for some buyers to secure a home. There were many companies who used to buy homes at slightly below market rate and re-sell them (on terms) greatly above market rate to buyers who struggled to get finance elsewhere. The buyers would pay a small deposit (as low as 5%) and agree to pay a higher interest rate. Payments – usually interest only – would continue for three to five years, whereupon, it was believed, the buyers would then qualify for traditional bank loans. These homes were known as "termies". Two large companies involved in such sales were Pax Properties and Jonray.

83. The idea of vendor finance is neither illegal nor unethical. Like many schemes where home buyers are given an opportunity, it is often misused. Dodgy operators are drawn to anything that makes it easy for them to earn large profits for little effort. In the 1990s and early 2000s, these vendor finance deals were known as "wraps". They were initially made popular by a property spruiker called Steve McKnight who wrote a book with the catchy title of *From 0 to 130 Properties in 3.5 Years*. It caught the attention of wanna-be property millionaires. The fact that McKnight owned zero properties at the time his book was published (admitted to this author) didn't bother him. What bothered many people, however, is that, as with most property gurus who claim to have "made money and now want to help others", their help comes at a price, usually thousands of dollars per person.

As another property spruiker, Dymphna Boholt, admitted (to this author): she didn't make millions of dollars until she started purporting to show others how to make millions of dollars. And, by using glowing testimonials (many of which were fake – and for which she faced stiff penalties which barely deterred her), she roped in thousands of hopeful millionaires thus enabling Ms Boholt to rake in many more millions of dollars.

Another spruiker, Rick Otton, claimed to be able to show people "how to buy property for just $1, with NO deposit and NO bank loan". Otton, who gave himself the laughingly absurd title of "Australia's Real Estate Consumer Advocate", soon attracted the attention of real consumer advocates. Following action by the erstwhile ACCC (Australian Competition and Consumer Commission) and the New South Wales Fair Trading, Otton received the biggest penalty in Australia's corporate history. In August 2017, the Federal Court ordered Otton to pay fines of $18 million for misleading and deceiving consumers. Despite many thousands of hopefuls paying Otton $3,000 each to attend his tell-all seminars and then $26,000 for his "mentorship programs", Otton reportedly filed for bankruptcy in 2020 (according to property journalist Jonathan Chancellor). In 2022, Sheree Becker, a real estate agent in Victoria and one of Otton's "students" (described as one of his protégés) who had paid Rick Otton tens of thousands of dollars to learn his "secrets", was jailed for three-and-a-half years for defrauding the ANZ bank. Becker's fall is indicative of the powerful seduction of the evil that exists in the real estate world. Be careful. Always remember Rule 1: OBEY THE LAW. The people to tell you whether you are breaking the law are lawyers, not spruikers or agents.

One of the most important real estate rules is: STAY AWAY FROM SPRUIKERS, no matter how tantalising their promises or how glowing their references. These are master con artists. Always get independent legal advice from a solicitor recommended by someone in whom you have complete trust (not a solicitor recommended by the spruiker or any person to whom you are paying money). Good legal advice can save your financial life.

84. When Geoff Lane sold his Roseville home in late 2023, his consideration towards the buyers saw him granted the right to stay in his home rent-free for several extra weeks. This enabled Geoff and his partner to move seamlessly into a new home, an apartment in nearby Chatswood. Such conciliatory and considerate arrangements are impossible at auction sales where the only thing on the mind of most agents is to make a sale as fast as possible. To such agents, price or terms are secondary to making a sale – at any price.

85. Author's personal research conducted regularly over many years. This figure is conservative. In some areas with some agents, 100 percent of homes are undersold.

86. To this author, the term "successful agent" refers to the integrity of the agent, the happiness of the agent's clients and the agent's negotiation skills. By these measurements, most agents would fail – indeed, they wouldn't make it past "integrity".

87. Readers of this book are welcome to use the Buyers' Price Declaration with attribution (to Michael Kies) when selling their own properties.

88. One of the most common questions asked of sales trainers is: "What do we do when sellers (or buyers) say they want to 'think it over'?" Most trainers sprout a number of lies, cliches or standard deceitful techniques, all aimed at making consumers "sign up" now. Of all the selfish methods taught to salespeople, this is one that I find the most abhorrent. As well as stupid. The best advice a good salesperson can ever give to serious

buyers or sellers is to THINK ABOUT IT. Not only is this almost always the right advice, it also causes the client to trust the salesperson.

Since my days as an agent, it has always amazed me how real estate networks have such slogans as "the right advice" (e.g. Ray White) yet they'd teach salespeople high pressure techniques to persuade sellers and buyers to act with scant thought. Maybe they meant the right advice for Ray White. Addendum: In 2023, the Ray White network (Head Office in Brisbane) paid six months' rent to assist a struggling migrant family who returned to the town of Biloela in Central Queensland. Ray White neither sought nor received publicity for their magnanimity which was offered freely and unconditionally. Both my wife and I – and the owners of the home (Frank and Jenny) – were deeply touched by this kindness. If only such culture could spread through the entire Ray White network.

89. https://youtu.be/UYspUO2dUpQ?si=6vPsK82nj0OQ3dn3. Or go to YouTube and search, "Dick Smith video on hotel booking agencies".

90. Some vendor advocates are excellent – especially those who make a huge effort to achieve two outcomes for the vendors: No risk of loss – therefore no upfront costs; together with the right to dismiss the agent if they act inappropriately – therefore no 'locked-in' contracts. The second outcome is to get you the best price. One way to determine the worth of a vendor advocate is to ask their opinion of selling by auction. If they recommend auction, reject them. Also, ask the vendor advocates if they are paid by agents as well as by you. Such instances are a classic conflict of interest. A vendor advocate who truly looks after your interest will not have multiple sources of income from looking after you – just one fee, the fee to support you.

91. The greatest let-downs in my business life have been agents to whom I have given my trust and then, later, they broke that trust. I never put my association with any agent ahead of what's right for the seller. As I said to Scott Kim recently, *"Sellers come first, friends come second. Maybe that's why I don't have many friends."* He laughed. I have lost many agents I considered friends. In Jenman Approved, we have expelled or refused to accept more agents than any group in the nation. Most real estate groups only require a pulse and the ability to pay their fees in order to join them. I am as confident as I have ever been about any agent that Scott Kim and his wife Mai Kim will hold true to the ethical values and the client care systems known as the "Jenman method". I hope that the Jenman family is associated with the Kim family for many years. And, of course, that our friendship continues to grow. I admire their courage and their inherent integrity.

92. Extract from lengthy (1,300 word) email sent by Scott Kim to author December 30, 2023. Scott gave many powerful examples on how correct staging increases the sale price of a home. Readers who wish to view the full email can contact support@jenman.com.au.

93. 52 Wilga Street, Mount Waverley. Says Scott Kim: *"We had two goes at selling this property. We first went onto the market, all original condition. The BEST we could achieve was $1,100,000. As the owners were on the verge of accepting, the father sadly passed away. The home was taken off the market while the family waited for probate. During this time, we offered to project manage a renovation. We renovated about 70% of the home and then styled it. After obtaining probate, we put it back onto the market in April 2023, and set a new record in the street when this home sold for $1,501,000, almost $400,000 MORE than the best offer before the renovation and styling. The cost of renovation and styling was $45,000."*

94. If any agent is receiving a commission for recommending that sellers spend money with that company, that's a clear conflict of interest. As happens with many agents with real estate advertising – the more the agent encourages the sellers to spend on advertising the more the agent pockets by way of kickbacks. Of course, the real estate industry does not like the word "kickbacks". It prefers the term "rebates" – just as the gambling industry prefers the word "gaming". But whatever way they try and spin it, being paid a commission removes any objectivity, even the appearance of objectivity. The best agents never accept money from outside companies in return for recommending their clients spend money with those companies. As well as wading through the fine print in the agent's Listing Agreement, sellers should ask the agent: "Are you being paid by the staging company? Or any other company or person to whom you are suggesting we pay money?" And please remember, staging companies require payment at the time you receive the benefit of their staging. It would be far too risky for them to accept payment when sold as the sellers will be long gone then.

95. McGrath Real Estate.

    FOOTNOTE: In another McGrath office, the agent offered to waive upfront advertising costs for sellers who came via Jenman. He said words to the effect of: *"For your sellers, Neil, I will be sure we treat them ethically."* He asked me not to publicise his name for fear of retribution from members of the franchise. As I ended the phone call, I said these words: *"I appreciate you agreeing to treat the Jenman sellers' ethically, but I have an idea for you that I am sure will greatly improve your sales results: Why don't you treat all your sellers ethically?"* He admitted he was not allowed to do such a thing. What a world when, to act ethically and in the best interests of clients, agents must do it in secret lest they get caught. As with most of my phone calls (especially with agents) this call was recorded (with disclosure). This point clearly shows that if sellers stand up to the agents, if they refuse to be controlled by the agents, the agents will allow the sellers to have control.

96. It cannot be stressed often enough, if you cannot find a good agent – one who will not seek to control you and one who has the skills to get you the best market price – then you will do just as well, often much better, selling without an agent. Soon, I plan to write a book called: *If You Can't Find a Good Agent, Sell Your Home Without an Agent*.

97. Brent Courtney died on May 22, 2022. He was 48. He was survived by his wife Sally and their three children, Ashton, Walker and Piper. Exactly a month earlier, on April 22, 2022, Brent sent me a text saying: *"How are you feeling?"* An agent who truly cared about others, a rare type of agent. He's sadly missed.

98. To qualify as a Jenman Approved agent, an agent must agree to release the seller from the Listing Agreement if so directed by Jenman Approved. The same condition virtually applies with agent suggested by Jenman Support. Whether they are Jenman Approved or not, they must agree, in the event of a dispute with the sellers, to abide by the decision of Neil Jenman or his representative. To be sure, in almost all cases, we rule in favour of the home seller not the agent – even when agents threaten to no longer do business with us. We do not want to business with agents who do not care about putting their clients' interests ahead of the agents' interests. No excuses, no exceptions.

99. Circa 2000. In his parliamentary office with his advisers.

100. Business Insider – Finance. *"Americans Still Delusional About The Value Of Their Homes"*. By Joe Wiesenthal. November 18, 2009.
101. Tom Panos.
102. Ibid 33.
103. The real estate industry does not have a name for the buyers' highest price. It only has a name for the sellers' lowest price – the reserve. However, smart and educated agents who have studied negotiation and perhaps read the same books as real estate consumers are reading are referring to the Buyers' Highest Price as "THE BHP".
104. By using a Buyers' Price Declaration. Refer to Caution Point 5 – Rules for Offers.
105. William Spencer Vickrey (1914–1996) was a Canadian/American professor of economics. Professor Vickrey won the Nobel Prize for Economics in 1996, a few days before his death. Professor Vickrey devised a method of auction where, unlike traditional methods of public auctions, buyers are compelled to pay their highest price. Essentially, he designed a sealed-bid method (with modifications) so that, as well as buyers being compelled to pay their highest price – and therefore the sellers receiving more than in a traditional auction – the buyers were also treated fairly. Any real estate agent who has studied the art of negotiation, especially the typical auction system, should have encountered Professor Vickrey and his method of getting a better price. Agents who have never heard of Professor Vickrey (which is most of them) have obviously not studied how to get the best price for their clients. How much more credibility is needed than to emulate a Nobel Prize winner. Agents are quick to knock "Jenman's ideas" but Jenman has merely done what he recommends all agents do – study negotiation and learn how to obtain the best price for home sellers. And that almost certainly means studying the work of the Nobel Prize winning economist Professor William Vickrey. Like much of what is recommended by Jenman, the Buyers' Price Declaration was not "invented" or even "designed" by Jenman. Rather it was discovered then recommended by Jenman.
106. It's obvious – when you think about it (which unfortunately many sellers don't before they sign up with an agent) – the worse the agent is likely to treat you, the more they need to control you – to lock you up with harsh contracts so that you can't escape for many weeks even months. If these agents didn't control sellers, they'd lose many (most) of their sellers as soon as the sellers started experiencing their conditioning, their low offers and the massive amount of money they are asked to pay in needless costs. A good agent, on the other hand, has nothing to fear. Good agents are confident their clients will be happy. Good agents treat their sellers well. Therefore, sellers stay with good agents; they don't want to leave. Hence the reason good agents don't need to control sellers to the extent that bad agents control sellers. As one rogue agent quipped: *"Without being controlled, most of our sellers would leave us as soon as we started conditioning them."*
107. Alexander Phillips, PPD Real Estate, Woollahra, NSW.
108. James Tostevin, Marshall White.
109. Jenny Facciolo – she and her husband, Frank, were selling their home in Kew.
110. Scott Kim of Scott Kim Real Estate, Mt Waverley, VIC (Disclosure: This is a Jenman Approved agency, one of which we are extremely proud).

111. Before deciding to "wait it out", you should make it clear that under no circumstances will you allow this agent to sell your home. The agent should release you immediately. After all, why make themselves even more disliked? Only the most churlish agents force sellers to wait until their time has expired before releasing the sellers. And, if they do release you, make sure they irrevocably agree that you are under no obligation of any kind – including financial. Ideally, consult your lawyer and have a formal release agreement prepared. A couple of hundred dollars is great value for peace of mind.

112. Anyone who knows world history knows that Russians are fearsome negotiators. During the Cuban Missile Crisis in 1962, former Secretary of State Dean Acheson told President Kennedy and his senior advisers: *"For the last fifteen years, I have fought here at this table alongside your predecessors in the struggle against the Soviet. Gentlemen, I do not wish to seem melodramatic, but I do wish to impress upon you one observation with all conceivable sincerity. A lesson I have learned with bitter tears and great sacrifice. The Soviet understands only one language: action. It respects only one word: force."* Text from the 2000 Movie 13 Days with actor Len Cariou in the role of Dean Acheson. Further information can be found in the book: *The Kremlin School of Negotiation* by Igor Ryzov.

113. Josh Tesolin.

114. So many agents now call themselves "the best" or "agent of the year" (a near meaningless award from a company they pay) that it's impossible to go into any area without seeing agents trumpeting themselves like rock stars. Indeed, there were more posters in Australian suburbs for real estate agents than for the 2024 Taylor Swift concerts.

115. This is how this agent – and thousands like him – win listings and control sellers.

116. From copy of the agent's Selling Agency Agreement provided to author.

117. From agent's email to sellers provided to the author.

118. Ibid.

119. As told to author.

120. Ibid 110.

121. Paul Barry.

122. Offering a guarantee to the sellers in my area was one of the best ideas I ever discovered in my real estate agency. Being the only agent in the area to offer a written service guarantee meant that my agency won hundreds of extra listings. Agents, I urge you to stop being so narrow and pessimistic, focused on worrying about what might go wrong if you hand control to the sellers instead of taking control. Sure, one or two may try and cheat you but most will admire you and seek you out.

ABOUT THE AUTHORS

Neil Jenman has worked in the real estate industry since 1972. Following the success of his own agency, he spent 25 years writing courses and advising agents how to succeed through focusing on the interests of clients.

Today Neil supports selected home sellers (as many as he can humanly help) through Jenman Support, a service helping real estate consumers.

Alec Jenman is Neil's son. In 2019, Alec finished his schooling. He is now fulfilling his childhood goal to emulate his father's ethical philosophy and passion for protecting honest real estate consumers. Alec has earned a senior role at Jenman Support.

Neil Jenman and his wife Reiden divide their time between their farm in Central Queensland (where Neil spent his teenage years) and their home in Melbourne.

Neil's passion is literature. He is a renowned scholar on the life and works of W. Somerset Maugham. Maugham once wrote: *"There is nothing more beautiful than goodness."*

Neil is deeply interested in Australian history, especially of life in the bush. He has had the privilege to assist Auda Maclean, a much-admired lady from his hometown who's writing a biography of her almost ten decades in the Central Queensland bush. Called *One Lifetime is Not Enough*, Auda's biography should be published in late 2024 or early 2025.

Neil is his happiest alongside his wife, Reiden, to whom he has been married since 1996.

And Alec is happiest when he is anywhere but Queensland.

PUBLICATIONS

Real Estate Mistakes

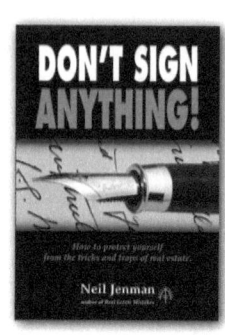

Don't Sign Anything!

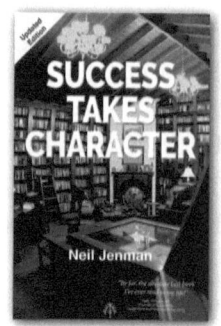

Success Takes Character

18 Worst Mistakes

13 Worst Mistakes

Help For Home-sellers

DOs and DON'Ts

42 Rules of Negotiation

88 Reasons

INDEX

8 Seller Protection Points Guarantee 146

42 Rules of Negotiation 39, 45, 64, 65, 105

88 Reasons Why You Must Never Auction Your Home 18

administration fees 28

advertising 15, 28
    conditioning, as a form of 99–100
    control strategy of REAs, as 49
    damaging value, when 58
    excessive, dangers of 49, 100
    find new leads for REA, as tool to 50
    franchise rules requiring premium, where 116–17
    included in commission, where 41
    payable whether a sale is achieved or not, where 94
    promotion of agent in 11, 40–1, 44, 49
    'puller ads' 58
    reasons REAs push 49–51
    sellers who refuse mass-marketing 54
    VPA (vendor paid advertising) 40–1, 47, 51, 54–5, 99
    without first contacting buyer contacts 44

advertising lemons 101

advice to agents 150–1

agenda of REAs 98–9

agent-finders 113–14

Angelou, Maya 78

asking price, setting too high xii, 61, 121–2

'auction lemons' 8, 100

auctions 8, 18, 30, 140, 146
    88 Reasons Why You Must Never Auction Your Home 18
    buyers attitudes towards 101
    clearance rates 100
    reasons agents push 30, 88, 99
    reserve price, pressure to lower 8, 110
    terms, no availability for 108

INDEX

bait-pricing 104

Bloomberg, Michael 129

bonus commission 29

building reports 78

buy first, sell later 119

buyers
    best paying, characteristics of 79
    circulation among many agents 45
    family-home buyers 60, 61
    fault-finders 60
    heart buyers 61
    investors 60–1
    myths about attracting 46
    negotiating with to obtain BHP 105–6, 110–11
    offerors distinguished 127
    terms or conditions, offering to 108–9

Buyers' Highest Price (BHP) 105
    negotiating to achieve 105–6, 110–11

Buyers' Price Declaration 105, 111, 139

buying for a low price
    putting effort into achieving 61

'buying the listing' 11

caution points
    agent-finders, avoid 113–14
    guarantee, insist upon 95–6
    hidden search prices 96–8
    offers *see* offers
    pause when stressed 112
    price delusion 121–2
    self-interest agenda of REA 98–9
    time trap 102
    'transparency trap' in negotiation 120–1
    unfair clauses in Selling Agency Agreements 94–5

caveat emptor 95

INDEX

caveat over home
    Selling Agency Agreements allowing agent to register 94, 139

commission, selling agents'
    bonus commission 29
    current average 6
    double commission, liability for 94–5
    negotiable until the point of sale 24, 26
    negotiating 23–29
    not payable when you find buyer yourself 11–12
    payable when sale is less than quoted price, where 94
    rates, range 28
    time for payment 2, 24
    time to negotiate 23

'company policy' excuse 27, 64

comparable sales 38

'conditioning' sellers down in price 5, 9, 14, 29, 87, 140
    comparable conditioning 38

consumer rights
    choice, right of 13
    informed, right to be 13
    redress or guarantee, right to 13, 95–6
    safety, right to 13

Continuing Agency Agreements 95

control vii, 134, 141, 149
    see also control the sale process, ways sellers can
    performance controls 2
    protection controls 2
    REAs over their clients vii, 141
    sale process, over xiii, 6

control the sale process, ways sellers can
    see also tips to achieve top result
    access to other agents, allowing 67–8
    agent's knowledge, test 30–3
    being informed 20
    'big brand' agents 68–9
    efficiency, encourage and reward 35–6

INDEX

    enthusiasm of REA, rating 59
    fair, firm and friendly behaviour 20–1
    'foreign agent', consider using 72, 128, 129
    'higher authority' rule, invoke 64
    highest price promise 74
    honest feedback 69–70
    inspections by pre-appointment only 66
    inspire agent, don't threaten 36–7
    keenness to sell, exhibit 21–2
    'love list', prepare 60, 106
    neighbours, do not overlook 62
    record conversations with the REA 70–1
    short-term selling agreements 34
    Sole Agency Agreements 62
    supporter or adviser 75
    take your time 72–3
    underselling, controlling 39, 73, 109–10
copywriting 28
Courtney, Brent 116

delayed settlement terms 108
do it yourself selling 15
Drucker, Peter 35

early access terms 108
early offers xii
elderly sellers 29
'endowment principle' 7
Exclusive Agency Agreements 12, 62
'extra charges' 28

fiduciary duty of REAs 133
firing your REA 139–41
For Sale signs 82–3

INDEX

Franklin, Ben 1, 88

gazumping 78
general listings 45
go-wrongs, allowing for 130
Golden Rule when selling 17, 59
good agents, recognising 16
    availability 90
    characteristics of 90–1
    chase up buyers 90–1, 101
    different than other agents 91
    knowledgeable 91
    personal attributes 16–17
    putting sellers' interests first 92
    questions to ask before signing 135–8
    risk, preparedness to accept 17, 91
    service guarantee, offering 96, 150
    Talk to People (TTP) 90
guarantee
agents who offer 18, 150
    right to 13, 95–6

hidden search prices 97–8
'higher authority' rule, invoke 64
houses on market for too long xii

Iles, Greg 134
illegal practices 104–5
indemnification clauses 95
independent legal advice
    Selling Agency Agreement, before signing 4, 64
inspections 15
    see also 'open houses'
    pre-appointment, by 66

INDEX

    REAs manipulating number of 84–5

Jenman, Alec x, 83, 95, 142, 148, 158
Jenman, Neil
    42 Rules of Negotiation 39, 45, 64, 65, 105
    88 Reasons Why You Must Never Auction Your Home 18
    advice to agents 150–1
    examples of REAs abusing his trust ix
    first agency ix
    protection of consumers xi
    testimonials from sellers 153–6
    The Real Estate Negotiation Course 65
Jenman, Reiden 157–8
Jenman Approved agents
    check with Jenman Support 118
Jenman philosophy 32
Jenman Support 62, 75–6, 83, 118, 142, 148
    joining the team 152
    website and telephone number 39, 45, 62, 65, 76, 83
Jenman System x
    Code of Client Care 117, 118
    Code of Ethics 117, 118

Karrass, Chester L 104
Kelly, Matthew 74
kickbacks to agent 94
Kies, Michael ix, 111, 128
'kill the sale' 25
Knopfler, Mark 43
knowledge viii, 149

Lane, Geoff 128, 145–7
Lanyon, Harold Edgar 157–8

INDEX

limit number of agents inspecting your property 124

'listen to the market' 47, 85

listing agreements see Selling Agency Agreements

local agents, prejudices of 72, 128, 129

'love list', prepare 60, 106

'low-balling' 12, 85
    dummy offers and 85

'lower your expectations' 128

lowest acceptable price
    do not disclose 22, 81

McKay, Maxwell Maurice 158

market appraisals 113

market forces 26

marketing costs 28
    see also advertising
    agent accepting risk for 17, 91
    payable on sale only 11
    payable whether a sale is achieved or not, where 94
    promotion of agent in 11, 40–1, 44, 49
    sellers who refuse mass-marketing 54
    time for payment 2
    VPA (vendor paid advertising) 40–1, 47, 51, 54–5, 99

Matthews, Debbie 158

'mystery shop' the REA 59, 132

negotiation
    privacy in, importance of 121
    transparency trap 120

negotiation skills 2, 15, 26
    The Real Estate Negotiation Course 65

neighbours, do not overlook 62

Nietzsche, Friedrich 96

INDEX

off-market sales 54–5, 56–7

offers
    acceptance of, question to answer 105
    be prepared to walk away 106
    off-the-cuff offers 107
    pressure, try to ignore 107
    REAs tactics to get sellers to accept 103, 105
    rules for 104–11
    take time to consider 103
    terms or conditions, offering 108–9
    threats, refuse to accept 106
    vendor finance 107–8

on-line auctions 120

'open houses'
    benefits to agents 66
    disadvantages to sellers 66–7
    identification of attendees 18
    leads for REAs, providing 35

open listings 45

patience, importance of 126–7, 140

pest reports 78

Pilger, John 31, 40

price confidence 87–8

price expectations xiii, 123

price quotes by agents 26
    forcing agents to honour 11
    REAs overstating 11, 113
    refusing to sell for price below 128

privacy 53, 121

prosecution of agents
    infrequency x

questions to ask REAs before signing 135–8

INDEX

quick sales 35–6

Rate-My-Agent 52

real estate agencies
    franchise rules requiring premium advertising, where 116–17
    hours of operation 59

real estate agents (REAs)
    buyer contacts 42, 43
    challenges for 5
    chasing buyers 90–1
    'conditioning' sellers down in price 5, 9, 14, 29, 87, 140
    dummy low-ball offers 85
    enthusiasm of 59
    essential knowledge required 33
    examples of abuse of trust by ix
    fake 'noise', creating 101
    finding sellers 5
    firing see firing your REA
    'friends' who are, using 133
    hard-working agents 89–90
    hidden search prices, use of 97–8
    inspection numbers, manipulating 84–5
    laziness 88–9
    making the sale 5
    negotiation skills 2
    overstating price quotes 8, 9, 113
    price-prejudiced 71
    questions to ask before signing 135–8
    self-interest agenda 98–9
    signing up sellers 5
    training, focus of 14, 32, 133
    under-quoting price to buyers 12
    unethical standards vii
    vulture agents 131–2

real estate industry
    distrust of, widespread 133
    interest of REAs, based on 99

INDEX

unethical standards vii

real estate websites
   hidden search prices 97–8
   search parameters 53

reserve price, pressure to lower 8

Rickenbacker, Eddie 72

risk
   good agents preparedness to accept 17, 91
   marketing costs, who bears the risk 42

safety 13, 53

sale process
   see also control the sale process, ways sellers can
   sale and purchase as one transaction 61

Salem Maskin, Jonathan 68

sell and buy simultaneously 119

sell first, buy later 119

sellers
   agents 'conditioning' down in price 5, 9, 14, 29, 87, 140
   rogue sellers 143
   sellers' lowest price 109
   testimonials from 153–6

selling
   Golden Rule 17, 59
   subject to sale 119–20
   'transference of enthusiasm', as 59

selling a secret 53–4, 56–7

Selling Agency Agreements vii
   advertising costs clauses 94
   agent indemnification clauses 95
   caveat over home, agent right to
   register 94, 139
   commission payable when sale is less than quoted price, where 94
   consequences of breaking, possible 8

INDEX

    Continuing Agency Agreements 95
    control clauses viii, 139
    Controlled Listing 139
    deletion of unfair clauses 95
    double commission, liability for 94–5
    Exclusive Agency Agreements 12, 62
    favourable clauses, adding 95
    forcing agents to release you 11
    independent legal advice before signing 4
    kickbacks to agent 94
    legally binding contract 3, 14
    liability to pay REA despite no sale, where 95
    long-term locked-in 2, 34, 94, 95
    rights to sell yourself are lost 94
    short-term selling agreements 34
    Sole Agency Agreements 62
    unfair conditions in 3, 94–5
    'upon demand' clauses 94

selling methods
    do it yourself 15, 142
    good agent, through 16
    typical agent, through 14

selling without an agent 6

Seneca 79

Service Guarantee 96, 150

Shev, Alec 64

Sole Agency Agreements 62

Somerset Maugham, William 41

staging or styling 115–16

stubborn sellers 61
    too high asking price xii, 61, 74

terms or conditions, offering buyers 108–9

threats, refuse to accept 106

time trap 102

INDEX

tips to achieve top result
- agent putting your interests first 92
- best paying buyers, focus on 79–80
- buyers already looking in the area 80
- buyers, treat kindly 78–9
- disclose information 78–9
- door-knockers, handle carefully 83–4
- entice an inspection 80
- For Sale signs 82–3
- hard-working agents, use 89–90
- lowest price, do not disclose 22, 81, 110
- negotiating too early, avoid 80
- over-selling, avoid 80
- price confidence 87–8
- protect the value of your property 85–6

transparency trap 120

Truman, Harry 133

trust ix, xi, 16, 75, 83, 104, 134
- examples of REAs abusing ix

underselling 28–29, 73, 109–10
- rate of undersold houses 38

unethical conduct
- REAs, by vii, 42, 44, 86, 132

United States
- multiple-listing network (MLS) 67

valuations 113

vendor disclosure 78–9

vendor finance 107–8

VPA (vendor paid advertising) 40–1, 47, 51, 54–5, 99
- agent promotion, as 40–1, 49
- up-selling trick 51–2

vulture agents 131–2

INDEX

Watkins, John 121
website
    jenman.com.au 39, 45, 62, 65
'What is the worst that can happen?' 3

www.ingramcontent.com/pod-product-compliance
Lightning Source LLC
Chambersburg PA
CBHW022221090526
44585CB00013BB/666